SiMPLE ACTS
The Busy Family's Guide to Giving Back

by Natalie Silverstein, MPH

Gryphon House
www.GryphonHouse.com

Published by Gryphon House, Inc.

P. O. Box 10, Lewisville, NC 27023

800.638.0928; 877.638.7576 [fax]

Visit us on the web at www.gryphonhouse.com.

Library of Congress Cataloging-in-Publication Data

The cataloging-in-publication data is registered with the Library of Congress for ISBN 978-0-87659-813-9.

Bulk Purchase

Gryphon House books are available for special premiums and sales promotions as well as for fund-raising use. Special editions or book excerpts also can be created to specifications. For details, call 800.638.0928.

Disclaimer

Gryphon House, Inc., cannot be held responsible for damage, mishap, or injury incurred during the use of or because of activities in this book. Appropriate and reasonable caution and adult supervision of children involved in activities and corresponding to the age and capability of each child involved are recommended at all times. Do not leave children unattended at any time. Observe safety and caution at all times.

Dedication

To Emi, Archie, and Alaina, whose kind hearts inspire me every day.

To Jenny Friedman, PhD, and the entire Doing Good Together team, for giving me an opportunity to pursue my passion for service and for providing the tools we all need to raise children who care and contribute.

To Jonathan, always.

Table of Contents

ACKNOWLEDGMENTS

This book is the result of a passion that evolved into a vocation. With some hard work, a little luck, and the support of many kind and generous people who believed in me, I was able to turn the dream of this book into reality.

Many thanks to Stephanie Roselli at Gryphon House for opening a plain brown envelope, addressed "To Whom It May Concern," and giving the contents a look and a chance. Thank you to my patient and kind editor, Candice Bellows, and the entire team at Gryphon House.

Thank you to Jenny Friedman for being a mentor and friend and for blazing a trail in this work that has inspired me since the moment I stumbled upon Doing Good Together.

To my Writer's Rock classmates—our thoughtful teacher, Alex; Candice, who invited me to join; Robyn; Michelle; Karen; and Kim—your writing makes me laugh through tears and reminds me how important it is to tell our stories. Thanks for keeping my chair warm.

Thank you to authors Elyssa Friedland and Lauren Brody, early champions whose enthusiasm for this concept encouraged me to persevere.

Everyone should be as lucky as I am to have two best friends and cheerleaders like Grace Idzal and Steffanie Levin. Your love and support sustain me, and I am grateful for you both, every day.

Emi, Archie, and Alaina—thank you for being my role models of kindness, gratitude, and empathy. Nothing makes me prouder than being your mom.

Thank you to Jonathan for everything. I love you.

Note: I will donate a portion of the proceeds from this book to Doing Good Together, a nonprofit organization.

INTRODUCTION:
THERE'S ALWAYS TIME TO GIVE BACK

"We don't wait to start reading to our children. We want reading to be a habit. Giving back is very much the same way. You're building that habit into your family when your children are very young."
—Jenny Friedman, PhD, founder and executive director of Doing Good Together

Kindness is easy. You don't need to have lots of leisure time or expendable resources, be a particular age, or live in a certain place to give back to your community. One of my favorite quotes about service is from Dr. Martin Luther King Jr., who said, "Everyone can be great, because anybody can serve." If you take a moment to look around, you will inevitably see someone who needs a little help or would be touched by a kind word or gesture. For me, Dr. King's quote speaks directly to children and families. I believe that everyone can and should find time to volunteer—even families with young children—in an age-appropriate and meaningful way. You just need to keep an open heart and a curious mind and to find the space in your busy schedule.

One of my family's favorite ways to do these things is to follow Dr. King's counsel on the American holiday named for him, the Martin Luther King Jr. Day of Service (popularly known simply as MLK Day). In addition to enjoying a day off from school and work, my family tries to make time to observe the "day of service" aspect of the holiday each year.

Several years ago, we had an opportunity to volunteer on MLK Day by serving a meal in a nearby soup kitchen, an effort sponsored by a local college. The facility only operates on Monday evenings and is typically staffed by students and faculty with help from volunteers. For MLK Day that year, our temple requested all of the volunteer spots,

SIMPLE ACTS

and families were encouraged to sign up. I was a little skeptical about doing so because my children were so young. Emilia ("Emi") would soon be thirteen, Archie was eleven, and Alaina was only six. Alaina was certainly too young to participate in a food-service activity, and I was unsure how much help she could be. But after inquiring about the age requirements, I was assured that all ages were welcome to help. So my husband, Jonathan, and I decided we would all go.

When the five of us arrived at the soup kitchen with the other volunteers, we received a brief orientation and job assignments. Emi and two friends were given the dual task of sorting donations (including socks, toothbrushes, soap, feminine-hygiene products, and clothing) and then distributing those items to guests as they departed the dining hall. For Emi, a young teen who loved clothes and shopping, this job was a perfect fit. She helped guests find clothing in the right sizes and pressed free toiletries upon everyone who passed.

Meanwhile, while Jonathan helped prepare the food, Archie set the tables and then, as is typical of boys that age, became a little bored and distracted during the meal service. He sat down at the piano, which dominated the center of the dining hall, and began to play the few pieces he had committed to memory from his lessons. It wasn't the New York Philharmonic, but people genuinely enjoyed hearing him play while they ate.

Little Alaina and I had the best job, and I was impressed with the creativity of the staff in placing us. We stood at the front door to greet the guests and check their bags, which presumably held all of their possessions. Alaina gave each person a claim ticket while I took bags and placed them behind our desk. Then Alaina, using a small tally counter, was thrilled to make a "click" for each person who passed through into the dining hall.

Our whole experience at the soup kitchen that evening took two and a half hours from start to finish. We were home in time for dinner, baths, and bed at a normal time. We still enjoyed our long weekend as a family, and the children still had a fun day off from school, but we were able to carve out a small piece of the day to do something helpful for a group of people living marginally in our city. A hot meal, a little music, a pair of clean socks, and a new toothbrush are all things my children take for granted on a daily basis. On that particular MLK Day, they had the satisfaction of easing the burden of a group of fellow New Yorkers by helping them enjoy an evening meal with dignity.

To Jonathan and me, service has always felt like an organic way to live our values, one of many tools we use in an attempt to raise kindhearted children. Long before our experience at the soup kitchen, I had begun searching for ways for us to serve as a family. However, despite living in a large city and being surrounded by people and organizations in need of help, I quickly learned that most nonprofits simply can't or won't accept young children as volunteers. My mission to seek family-friendly volunteer opportunities was born.

Over the years, my search continued to widen until I discovered Doing Good Together. Founded in 2004, Doing Good Together is a national nonprofit located in Minneapolis–St. Paul, Minnesota, that provides tools to help parents raise children who care and contribute. Over the last five years, Doing Good Together has expanded to additional urban areas across the United States and reaches a broad national audience through a robust website that is full of resources and inspiration. I became the New York City–area coordinator for Doing Good Together, and through this role, I can pursue my passion for service as I continue to hone my expertise in family-friendly volunteerism and share it with others. I now curate and publish a monthly listing of family-friendly service opportunities in the New York City region and am a frequent speaker and writer on the subject.

Even outside of work, I am constantly involved in promoting volunteerism. Scarcely a week goes by without parents reaching out to me personally and asking for a community-service project idea for a child's birthday, an upcoming holiday, a life event, or simply a way to cultivate kindness and generosity in their family. I've become a resource for many people on the topic of family service, counseling individuals and organizations and providing ideas, tips, and suggestions. This work has enriched my life, introduced me to many like-minded parents, and solidified my belief that engaging in service as a family is vitally important to raising kind and grateful children.

Why Serving with Your Children Matters

We live in a complicated, increasingly disconnected society. So many things that were invented to connect us—the internet, electronic devices, social media, and more—sometimes isolate us from each other and, unfortunately, stir up difficult parenting issues. We are challenged to explain senseless violence, cynicism, hurtful speech, and negative messages. We need to interpret inequity and tragedy for our children, even when we don't understand these things ourselves. I think we are all searching for tools to empower our children to be hopeful and make a positive impact on the world. Volunteering as a family is one simple answer: a proven way to foster compassion, empathy, kindness, and tolerance in our children.

This is not wishful thinking—volunteering is not just a "nice" thing to do. Engaging in community service in childhood and, more specifically, volunteering as a family has a meaningful, long-term impact on children. For example, the Harvard Graduate School of Education embarked on the Making Caring Common Project in 2014 and since then has conducted research, launched media campaigns, and continued to provide resources to help parents raise children who are caring, responsible to their communities, and committed to social justice. The project researchers found that, just as in learning to play an instrument or honing a craft, children need to practice caring and helpfulness with guidance from adults. Daily repetition forms habits of kindness and makes caring second nature.

The idea for *Simple Acts* came from an exchange with a friend who complimented my commitment to engaging in service with my children as she lamented her own inability to find time to do so with her two young boys. I assured her that it didn't need to be a big, time-consuming effort. I suggested that she and her family could find one activity to do together each month, but she cut me off with a gasp: "Once a *month*? Are you crazy?" She said she wished she could commit to service even once a month, but with the endless list of activities consuming her children's after-school and weekend hours—sports, piano lessons, tutoring, swimming, the list goes on and on—it seemed impossible to fit it in.

It's interesting that we manage to find time for all of these other commitments in our children's lives, yet the activities that would most help to build character, resilience, patience, and gratitude—the values we all say we cherish—are the ones we can't or won't prioritize. Ultimately, saying yes to volunteering means saying no to something else, and that can be a difficult choice for parents to make. Perhaps it means saying no to an academic tutoring session or an additional piano lesson or an athletic outing—all important activities that will help a child succeed as he pursues a passion. However, the argument could be made that serving others, developing empathy and gratitude, and cultivating tolerance are just as important. The Making Caring Common Project highlights this gap between rhetoric and reality. The researchers found that parents *say* that their highest priority is building habits of caring and compassion, qualities that they rank as more important than their children's achievements. But the data indicates that "youth aren't buying it." The majority of the young people surveyed said that their parents are more concerned about achievement—academic or extracurricular—than about caring for others.

I have found this pattern to be true in my own interactions with parents. When I speak to groups about the importance of volunteering with their children, there are always many nodding heads and smiles of affirmation. One-on-one, however, parents express frustration and resignation, throwing up their hands at their inability to find the time for service in busy family schedules. Or, if they do have the time, they simply don't know where to find age-appropriate, convenient, and compelling service opportunities in their communities.

The goal of this book is to overcome that challenge. It is important to note that *Simple Acts* is *not* a to-do list. You need not approach the chapters in a linear fashion or follow each suggestion exactly. This book is meant to provide a wide assortment of unique and compelling tools, along with (hopefully) inspiring stories, to spark your imagination as you consider service and how it relates to your busy family's life. You can use as many ideas as you like, focusing on the ones that connect with your interests, and do so using whatever order and timeline make sense for your family. If your children are very young, you may be initiating these activities on their behalf, but this doesn't diminish the impact. Children see what you do and hear what you say when you interact with others, and every observed act of compassion and generosity will be stored away in your children's experiences and will help to shape their values and character.

It's Easier Than You Think

Throughout this book, you'll find suggestions and links to help you identify nonprofits in your local community and across the country that relate to a particular event, activity, or interest. In addition to Doing Good Together—which publishes local listings of family-friendly volunteer opportunities in six cities: Minneapolis, St. Paul, New York, Baltimore, Boston, Seattle, and Silicon Valley—there are other organizations all over the United States focused on promoting family service. The Resource Guide at the end of this book provides a list of these national resources, as well as comparable organizations in every state that can help you discover volunteer opportunities in your area. A quick internet search will often bring up additional resources. Helpful search terms include "family volunteering in [your city/state]," "family-friendly volunteer opportunities," "volunteering with children," and "youth volunteer opportunities."

But don't stop with this book when looking for places to serve. Network with your friends and neighbors who have volunteered. Keep your ears open for people sharing positive service experiences. And once you've discovered a welcoming place to volunteer with children, share it! Other parents will want to hear about it.

When you've identified organizations of interest, be sure to do a little research. You would never accept a paid position at a company you had not vetted thoroughly, and the same rules should apply for volunteer jobs, especially if you are bringing your young children along. Use these steps to check whether a particular organization is the right fit for your family:

- Navigate the organization's website (if there is one). Does it offer specific information about how to volunteer, the types of activities, and whom to contact for more information? Does it include testimonials from other volunteers?
- Check the website to see if the organization is rated by Charity Navigator (typically shown at the bottom of the home page). Charity Navigator has been administering a rating system of nonprofits for more than fifteen years. While the focus of Charity Navigator is to help donors identify the best organizations to support with philanthropic dollars, it does offer information on volunteering. A favorable Charity Navigator rating is a good indication that the organization is well managed and effective in achieving its mission.
- Identify a volunteer coordinator or executive director, and contact her to ask questions about the volunteer opportunities being offered and any training being provided to volunteers.

- Observe how quickly the organization responds to your inquiry and how forthcoming they are with information. You'll get a sense immediately if there is a welcoming culture and a joyful pursuit of the organization's mission and if it is a place where your family will feel comfortable.
- Make sure that the organization maintains insurance and that all volunteer activities are supervised appropriately.
- Be sure that the organization's mission is in line with your family's values and that the work you will be doing matches your interests. Young children are more likely to be excited about volunteering and to remain engaged during the activity if it relates to an issue you've discussed as a family or they've explored in school.
- If your children are very young, it's a good idea to make sure that the volunteer activity will only last an hour or two. Young children's attention spans are short, and you want everyone to finish with a smile.

Little Hands Can Help, Too

Many parents ask, "I'd love to serve with my family, but are my children too young? I thought most nonprofits only welcome adult volunteers." This is probably the biggest stumbling block for parents. In my experience, however, even very young children can engage in hands-on service in their communities—and *everyone*, no matter what age, can have fun with kindness activities at home. If you make the effort to find the time and the means, there is always something you can do.

It is important for parents to understand the age requirements for any volunteer opportunity. Many organizations arbitrarily set a minimum age of fourteen or sixteen, while others insist that all volunteers be adults. Of course, certain types of organizations (for example, those that serve the mentally ill or the incarcerated) can only accept adult volunteers for safety and liability reasons. However, many nonprofits will state that volunteers must be a certain age, but when specifically asked about younger children, they will acknowledge that children are welcome with an adult who will closely supervise them, sign a waiver, or both. If you are interested in volunteering somewhere with your children, don't be discouraged if they don't meet a specified age requirement. Just ask. You'll be surprised at how many organizations will allow children under certain circumstances.

Making It Meaningful

Once you and your family have found a place to volunteer, how will you get the most out of the opportunity? Each chapter in this book includes suggestions to help your family set goals for specific experiences, maximize your time, make the effort meaningful, and reflect on your service. For example, Jenny Friedman, PhD, and Jolene Roehlkepartain share seven keys to a successful family service project in their book *Doing Good Together: 101 Easy, Meaningful Service Projects for Families, Schools and Communities*:

1. **Purpose:** Look around your neighborhood, community, or city to identify immediate or persistent needs, or talk with your children in an age-appropriate way about issues of national or global concern. Identify an issue that speaks to your hearts, and seek a way to act.

2. **Simplicity:** Keep the concepts, the activity, and the conversation simple for young children. If you can, use a related children's book or conversation-starter question to frame the activity. The Doing Good Together website (https://www.doinggoodtogether.org) offers a "Reading with Empathy" section listing children's books that you can use to spark conversations about service and social-justice issues. (See the Resource Guide at the end of this book for more information.)

3. **Creativity:** Children are always more engaged if an activity involves a creative, active element, such as arts and crafts, drawing, music, games, movement, gardening, filling bags, or wrapping boxes—anything that uses their hands and imaginations.

4. **Intergenerational appeal:** The activity should appeal to children of all ages, as well as the adults in your family or group.

5. **Relationship building:** Ideally, you and your children will interact directly with the recipient of your good works. While that's not always possible, building a relationship with the clients, leadership, or other volunteers makes every outing more effective and special.

6. **Reflection:** Take time during and especially after the activity or event to reflect on what you and your children observed, how you felt, and what you learned. I have suggested sample reflection questions at the end of each chapter, and Doing Good Together offers reflection questions and ideas on its website.

7. **Next steps:** Think about ways you can continue to engage with the organization, person, or group you helped. Service is particularly meaningful when it becomes a tradition and is woven into the fabric of family life on an ongoing basis.

There are no secret tricks for creating and maintaining a lifelong practice of kindness and service with your children. Just stay positive and flexible, roll with the inevitable glitches, and most importantly, make it fun. Keep smiling, and remember that by doing so you are showing your children that helping others makes you, the givers, feel really good, too.

Final Words of Inspiration Before You Get Started

Volunteering together is good for children and for families. Regardless of the work that is accomplished in each individual activity, the effort that is expended and the time spent are thoroughly worthwhile. You don't need to change the world to make a difference. Every act, no matter how small, accumulates like drops of rainwater collecting in a bucket. Each time your family considers issues and takes action, you are contributing positive experiences to your children's developing character. You are acting locally—

perhaps hyperlocally by doing kindness activities at your kitchen table—but you are affecting others in a meaningful way, sending ripples of goodness outward, and letting your children absorb the positive response. Without fanfare or self-congratulation, you are quietly and consistently living your family's values.

In my experience, family service does have a meaningful impact on children as they grow. Volunteering together creates warm family memories and traditions, and it engenders empathy and gratitude in children. Not every outing will be perfect, of course. Life can be messy, people are unpredictable, and sometimes things don't work out as planned. The mind-set, the effort, and the sincere positive intention are what will remain with your children after they have grown up and headed off on their own to make an impact on the world.

I believe you will never regret doing something nice for another person. That person may not remember you. She may not even seem to acknowledge or appreciate your kindness, but you'll still be glad to have helped. I am convinced that all parents believe this and instinctively understand the benefits of starting kindness habits when children are very young, as the children's personalities and core values are being established. Parents simply don't know where to begin. I hope this guide will provide the inspiration and tools parents need to fit service into busy family lives.

CHAPTER **ONE**
Organizing Playdates with Purpose

> "Alone we can do so little; together we can do so much."
> —Helen Keller, American author and activist

After-school or weekend playdates are a frequent activity in early childhood and provide a perfect place to begin our discussion of incorporating simple acts of kindness into busy schedules. I have spent a considerable amount of time over the years arranging, hosting, and shuttling my three children around to play with friends. My oldest, Emi, was even a bit of a playdate tyrant. I would arrive at nursery school to collect her, anxiously anticipating hugs and sticky kisses, but before I could ask about the many details of her day, she would urgently ask me, "Do I have a playdate?" It wasn't a pleasant scene if I had forgotten to arrange one.

These coordinated social interactions are important for young children as their personalities and temperaments begin to develop and they embark on the lifelong process of learning how to share, resolve conflict, and navigate human interaction. While unstructured playtime is encouraged, sometimes a specific kindness activity or outing will keep little ones engaged while imparting lessons about working together to care for others.

When incorporating service into a playdate, there are many creative options that you can adjust to the ages and attention spans of the children, the season, the weather, and the amount of time you want to spend on service while still allowing time for free play. It's important for the adults to roll with any unforeseen glitches and to show a healthy dose of enthusiasm to get the children excited about participating. If everything doesn't go smoothly the first time, try again. Raising kindhearted children is a marathon, not a sprint. Every small effort is worthwhile, and even if one activity flops, the next one might be a big hit. The important thing is to keep trying in a low-key, organic, and positive way.

Tips for Holding a Playdate with Purpose

The possibilities are endless, but use these simple tips to plan a successful playdate with purpose:

- Start with a story.
- Keep it simple, creative, and fun.
- Share, reflect, and keep it going.

The rest of this chapter explains and gives ideas for each of these steps.

Read a Book to Set the Stage

If you are hosting a playdate with purpose, it's important to set a positive tone and engage young children right away. One of the best ways to do this is by reading a story together. Before you begin a kindness activity at home or head out into the neighborhood to do a service project, sit together and read an age-appropriate children's book to frame the experience. Books such as *Those Shoes* by Marybeth Boelts, *The Last Stop on Market Street* by Matt de la Peña, *Somebody Loves You, Mr. Hatch* by Eileen Spinelli, and *Ordinary Mary's Extraordinary Deed* by Emily Pearson are some of my favorites. But there are many wonderful books about generosity and making a difference, as well as others that deal with social-justice themes in a gentle way for young children. You can also find many resources online that provide topical lists to help you identify stories that will make your efforts more accessible for young children and will spark important conversations and reflection. Here are some of these resources:

- The Doing Good Together website (https://www.doinggoodtogether.org) features a "Reading with Empathy" section, which offers a list of books that cover a range of issues. (See the Resource Guide for more information.)
- Read Brightly (www.readbrightly.com) is an online resource featuring book recommendations, reading tips, and seasonal inspiration to help parents and educators grow lifelong readers. It offers lists of recommended books about service, kindness, and social-justice themes.
- The Best Children's Books (www.the-best-childrens-books.org) is a website created by teachers that offers lists of the best children's books by subject. You can find book suggestions covering topics such as generosity, honesty, gratitude, and open-mindedness.
- A quick internet search will uncover many parenting blogs with lists of children's books about service, kindness, and current social issues.
- Bookstores often group and display children's books by theme, especially around holidays such as the Martin Luther King Jr. Day of Service, Valentine's Day, Independence Day, and Thanksgiving.

Keep It Simple, Creative, and Fun

Young children love to be creative and messy when playing together. Coloring, arts-and-crafts projects, and baking are great playdate activities. While free play should be encouraged, a little bit of directed activity can open up natural conversations about generosity, gratitude, and compassion.

The next several sections include ideas for projects that you can complete at home or in the community, including a larger-scale idea for bigger groups. For maximum enjoyment and learning, choose activities that appeal to both the children and their families or caregivers.

 Quick Kindness Tip: Choosing an Organization to Support

Many of the suggestions in this chapter refer to national organizations that encourage donations and include detailed instructions on their websites. However, before beginning an at-home kindness project, think about the organizations or people in your own community to whom you might send or deliver the things you make. It's always a good idea to make a connection with these organizations in advance to talk about the items you'd like to donate and to ensure that these gifts are welcome, safe, and acceptable for the intended recipients. During these conversations, you might learn about an alternative or additional project that would be fun for the children to do and would provide something needed by the agency. For example, you might be thinking of making lap blankets for the elderly in a local nursing home. But while talking with the volunteer coordinator, you learn that many of the seniors receive no mail and have bare bulletin boards in their rooms, so they might prefer cheerful drawings and cards instead.

Do-at-Home Service Ideas for Playdates
Make Cards and Letters of Encouragement and Gratitude

You don't need much to spread some joy—just paper and crayons, markers, or colored pencils.

- Make "Welcome Home" posters for active-duty military through Operation Help a Hero (https://www.operationhelpahero.org). Operation Help a Hero coordinates support for soldiers and military families, including celebrations when soldiers return to their home barracks after deployment. "Welcome Home" posters, along with cards and gifts, toiletries, snacks, and other treats, are given to soldiers to show appreciation and provide a warm welcome upon their return.
- Senior citizens who live in a local nursing home or assisted-living facility may not receive a lot of visitors or mail. Children can create cheerful cards with simple messages such as "thinking of you" to cheer the elderly or infirm. If the playdate

takes place close to a holiday, applicable greetings can be included. Contact the nursing home or facility to find a convenient time to deliver your cards.

- Make cards for children who are ill, disabled, or traumatized, and donate them to your local children's hospital or cancer center. If your community doesn't have these facilities, try making cards for one of these organizations:
    - Send Kids the World (www.sendkidstheworld.com) allows you to search a list of children who are battling serious illnesses and to direct encouraging cards, letters, and postcards to a particular child.
    - Cards for Hospitalized Kids (www.cardsforhospitalizedkids.com) offers a similar database and provides helpful information to make this activity a success, including a checklist for hosting a card-making event or playdate.
    - The Confetti Foundation (http://confettifoundation.org) supplies party kits to children who spend their birthdays in the hospital. Each kit includes a handmade birthday card (see "Adding Kindness to Any Party" in chapter 2).
- Many nonprofit organizations that address hunger through home delivery of nutritious food, such as Meals on Wheels (https://www.mealsonwheelsamerica.org), include handmade cards in delivery packages and gladly accept donations all year long. The cards can be general notes of encouragement, birthday cards, or holiday greetings.

 Quick Kindness Tip: Make Cards at Mealtimes

Always keep a stack of construction paper (folded into cards) and a bucket of crayons, markers, or colored pencils on the dining table or within arm's reach of where children eat meals. While waiting for food to be served or after helping to clear dishes, you can encourage your children to create cheerful cards for soldiers, senior citizens, or children battling serious illnesses.

Make Bird or Squirrel Feeders

Kindness and caring should extend to the natural world. Create a homemade bird or squirrel feeder for your backyard animal friends. Here are a few simple examples:

- String pieces of round oat cereal onto pipe cleaners, and bend them into heart shapes.
- Fill the crevices of a pinecone with peanut or almond butter, and roll the cone in birdseed. Hang it outside a window with string or wire. Alternatively, use a cardboard tube instead of a pinecone, and string it on wire or yarn between two branches of a tree.
- Fill a mason jar or a painted tin can halfway with birdseed, crumbs, cereal, or scraps of bread. Lay the container on its side on a windowsill.

Create Drawings and Paper Flowers

- Create colorful drawings or simple tissue-paper flowers to deliver to your local senior center or nursing home. The flowers can be inserted into small flowerpots or paper cups that are decorated with paint or stickers. Follow these basic steps to make the flowers:
    1. Stack several square sheets of colorful tissue paper on top of each other.
    2. Fold the stack accordion style.
    3. Round the ends with scissors (optional).
    4. Use wire or a pipe cleaner to make the stem, wrapping one end around the center of the accordion.
    5. Spread out the individual folds of tissue paper to create petals.
- Download printable coloring sheets from Color A Smile (https://colorasmileorg. presencehost.net/), a nonprofit that distributes drawings to senior citizens, hospitalized children, soldiers overseas, or anywhere a smile is needed. Detailed instructions are provided on the website.

Cook or Bake

- Baking and decorating treats (and taste-testing the finished products, of course) is always a fun activity with children. Cookies or muffins can be delivered, along with a note of gratitude, to your local firehouse or police precinct, where children may get to explore a fire truck or tour the station.
- Leave a ziplock bag of baked treats in your mailbox as a surprise for the mail carrier. If you are expecting a large package, do the same for the delivery driver by leaving a treat bag at your front door.
- Deliver baked treats to an elderly or ill neighbor with a cheerful note. Or, if you are feeling really ambitious, consider cooking a meal or making soup to deliver at dinner time.

Make Pet Toys

Make pet toys for donation to the ASCPA or your local animal shelter. Even young children can make chew toys out of supplies you likely have around the house—scraps of fabric and fleece, old T-shirts or socks, tennis balls, and empty water bottles. Here are a few simple examples:

- Wrap an empty plastic water bottle in a piece of an old T-shirt, and knot or braid the ends. Dogs love the crinkly sound the bottle makes.
- Insert a tennis ball into a colorful old sock, and knot the end.
- Braid several long scraps of fleece into a thick, short rope, and knot both ends.

Decorate Lunch Bags and Place Mats

Decorate paper lunch bags or plain place mats for donation to your local food pantry, Meals on Wheels program, or other food-delivery network. These organizations typically welcome these items, along with handmade birthday cards, to include in food-delivery packages to brighten the recipients' days.

Craft No-Sew Fleece Blankets

Make no-sew fleece blankets for donation to residents at a senior center, children in the hospital, or children in a shelter or foster care. You'll need a few yards of colorful fleece and scissors. This project is best done with children who can tie knots on their own.

1. Cut two large squares of fleece (about 1 ½ yards x 1 ½ yards each).
2. Place the squares back-to-back. If a design is only printed on one side, be sure the sides with the design are facing out.
3. At each corner, cut off a 3" x 3" square, cutting through both pieces of fleece. This forms the corners of the blanket.
4. Starting about 1" past the first corner, cut roughly 1" x 3" strips through both pieces of fleece all along the edges of the squares.
5. Tie the strips together (always use one strip from the top piece and one strip from the bottom piece) so that the blanket is surrounded by knots on all four sides.

 Quick Kindness Tip: Kindness Craft Kits

Some companies sell kindness-themed arts-and-crafts projects. If you keep a few of these kits on hand, they provide ready-to-use craft projects for a playdate.

- Stars of Hope (http://starsofhopeusa.org) is a program of the New York Says Thank You (NYSTY) Foundation, an organization that was created after the terrorist attacks of September 11, 2001. NYSTY mobilizes volunteers, many of whom are NYC firefighters and first responders, to travel around the country helping communities that have been touched by tragedy or natural disasters (hurricanes, tornados, wildfires, and so on). The Stars of Hope program grew out of this work, as volunteers would decorate wooden stars with positive, hopeful messages and hang them from trees and fences around areas struggling to recover. A Box of Hope includes fifteen precut wooden stars, acrylic paints, brushes, instructions, and a reusable box so you can ship the completed stars to a community in need of support.
- Little Loving Hands (https://www.littlelovinghands.com) offers a subscription service, delivering a kindness craft kit every month. Each box contains information so that your children can learn whom, why, and how they are helping, as well as a prepaid envelope to send the completed craft to someone in need.
- Craft-tastic Kits from the Ann Williams Group (https://www.annwilliamsgroup.com) offers a few craft activities that make excellent kindness projects.

Make Sandwiches for the Homeless

Identify a local homeless-outreach organization, and contact the director to ask whether the organization would accept a donation of individually wrapped sandwiches. Putting together sandwiches in an assembly line is a fun activity for young children. Each sandwich can be packaged in a plastic bag and placed in a predecorated paper bag along with a handmade note of encouragement.

Start a Giving Box or Jar

Make a giving box (or jar) using any material you like, such as a mason jar, coffee can, or shoebox. Let the children decorate the box with markers, stickers, glue, and wrapping paper. Talk to the children about how they might collect spare change from family on a regular basis, and ask what charities they would like to support with the collected money. *How the Moonjar Was Made* by Eulalie Scandiuzzi is a perfect children's book to read as part of this project.

Make Friendship Bracelets

Even young children can learn simple braids and "stitches" to create friendship bracelets out of lanyard or string and, if desired, beads. Tutorials for friendship bracelets can be found online. Instead of having children simply exchange bracelets with their best buddies on the playdate, encourage them to also make bracelets for new students at school or for children that they've noticed sitting alone at lunch or recess.

Assemble Activity Kits for Children in the Hospital

If the children on your playdate like working with beads, give them the tools to create activity kits for children who are in the hospital and in need of diversion and stimulating activity. For each kit, place twenty-five multicolored beads and about eight inches of stretchy string in a snack-size ziplock bag. Include a note or a label on each baggie with well wishes for the recipient and instructions for making the bracelets.

Community-Service Ideas for Playdates

You don't need to spend money on movies, bowling, arts-and-crafts studios, or drop-in music classes to keep children happy on a playdate away from home. There are lots of fun ways to go on free, easy, and meaningful "kindness outings" in your neighborhood.

Deliver the Good Stuff You've Made!

Making and delivering items can be parts of the same playdate, or you can make items during one playdate (or at another time with your family) and deliver them during another playdate. Delivery outings require a little prep work in advance, as you may need to contact the recipients (whether they are individuals or organizations) to be sure someone will be available to accept your gifts during the time you have planned to visit. Many organizations are always open and will likely welcome you if you drop by. For example, my family lives next door to an assisted-living facility, and there is always someone at the front desk to greet us and accept a stack of cheerful cards that we've made on a playdate.

Visit a Homebound Person, Nursing Home, or Senior Center

Researcher Joyce Varner has studied residents in nursing homes. Her work has shown that up to 60 percent of nursing-home residents in the United States receive no personal visits from family or friends. Senior adults, particularly those who are homebound or living in a residential facility, are often lonely and would be delighted by the company of children. Intergenerational friendships benefit young and old alike. A visit to a homebound neighbor or a local nursing home is a great way to make seniors feel remembered and respected. These visits can also help children hone their skills in empathetic listening and patience.

Most senior facilities have an activities coordinator, resident-life manager, or other administrative professional who monitors and schedules visitors, guests, and groups. You can check the organization's website or call its main number to reach the appropriate person, who can help you coordinate a visit during a convenient time and make sure that your proposed activities and gifts are acceptable. If you are able to visit, try some of these activities.

- Distribute cards, drawings, or paper flowers.
- Sing songs or initiate a sing-along with the seniors. Suggest simple, familiar tunes so that everyone will feel comfortable joining in. Bring along small handheld instruments such as egg shakers.
- If the seniors are agreeable, bring a small speaker to play music, and host a dance party.
- If the facility will allow it, bring along your gentle dog or cat. Therapeutic pet visits are often encouraged.
- Offer to organize a bingo game.
- Bring crayons and paper or printed coloring sheets, and create art with the seniors.

Plan a "Full Circle" Outing

I have to credit my children's Reform Jewish elementary school in New York City for this meaningful service-learning project. Throughout their first-grade year, children are asked to bring in spare change and add it to the classroom *tzedakah* (charitable collection) box every Friday. At the end of the semester, several field trips are planned. First, the children bring the collected change to a local bank and exchange it for paper money. The money is then split evenly among groups of children. A second field trip takes the class to the supermarket with a list, provided by a local food pantry, of nonperishable items. The children figure out what they can purchase with the money they are allotted. It's a meaningful lesson in thoughtfully shopping and working within a budget. From there, the class visits the local food pantry. They deliver the groceries and take a tour of the facility. Staff members tell them about pantry operations, the people being served, and the other resources that are offered to clients. The visit concludes with the children working together to assemble small bags of rice or beans from the industrial-sized bags that are donated by corporations. This project teaches concepts from many content areas—math, civics, budgeting, social justice, and hands-on service—as children learn about hunger and food insecurity in a tangible, relatable way.

You can try a similar activity with one or two children or a larger group on a playdate.

- If you'd like to make this a longer-term project, ask the parents of your children's friends to collect spare change for a few weeks prior to the date of the outing.
- Contact your local food pantry in advance to set up a convenient time for your visit. You may wish to split this activity over two playdates, visiting the supermarket on the first playdate and the food pantry on the second.
- Whether the children come with collected money or you offer each child a few dollars with which to shop, visit the supermarket and provide the children with a short list of nonperishable items to find.
- During your visit to the food pantry, ask whether the children can help stock the shelves with their donated items or assist with other simple tasks. Be sure to ask an employee or volunteer to talk to the children about the work the pantry does and the people it serves.

Help Mother Earth

One of the best ways to engage children in service, no matter the climate or the season, is to take them to places outside where they can enjoy nature, get dirty, and think about the many ways that we can care for the earth. On a playdate, children can do many small actions to help the environment and their neighbors.

- Use a children's book such as *365 Ways to Live Green for Kids* by Sheri Amsel to frame your conversation around "green" playdate activities.
- A community garden is a wonderful oasis in many cities, and volunteers of all ages are typically welcome to contribute to the upkeep of the garden. Even very young children can help to harvest vegetables, rake, spread mulch, or water the plants.
- Community-supported agriculture (CSA) is a model of sustainable farming that is helping small farms thrive in a difficult business. Farms in this model offer "shares"— portions of fruit and vegetables from the harvest—to local residents in exchange for a small payment. Many CSA farms welcome volunteer help from local residents and shareholders, especially during harvest season. If you live near a CSA farm, reach out to ask whether you and your children can volunteer there.
- For walks around your neighborhood or to and from a playdate, consider taking a small trash bag along and encouraging children to pick up and discard any trash they find. Children can wear gardening or latex gloves for safety and hygiene. Many larger municipal parks and green spaces encourage this type of impromptu cleanup and may offer bags, tools, and gloves. For example, Central Park in New York City (http://www.centralparknyc.org) offers an ongoing Pitch In, Pick Up effort all across the 840-acre park.

- If you live in a climate with frequent snow days, your children will likely get together with friends to sled, build snowmen, and play during each day off from school. While children are outdoors playing after a snowstorm, encourage them to help shovel snow and spread salt on the front walk or porch of an elderly or ill neighbor.
- Start a recycling drive in your neighborhood, apartment building, or community center. The children can decorate boxes for collecting plastic bottles or aluminum cans, along with signs encouraging donations.

Spread Joy with Sidewalk Chalk

In my neighborhood in New York City, an anonymous artist leaves positive, hopeful quotes and messages in sidewalk chalk in front of businesses and on street corners. Often I'll stop in my tracks to read a message, and it will brighten my day. Sometimes the messages relate to an upcoming holiday, but typically they are just happy thoughts for people who spend so much of their time rushing around with their eyes cast down.

Children can draw colorful designs, such as hearts, smiley faces, rainbows, and stars, and can write happy, hopeful messages along the sidewalk in front of your home or on your driveway for others to see while walking or driving by. With permission, children can create similar messages in front of the homes of neighbors or friends or the entrances to local businesses. If your children do not yet know how to write, they can color in a shape outline you've drawn, and you can work together on the written message.

Large-Scale Service Playdate: Park Cleanup and Picnic

Many playdates involve just two families. But occasionally you may want to include several families and take on a larger project. This section provides ideas for how to organize and execute a park cleanup and picnic, but you can also use these tips to set up other large-group service playdates.

No matter where you live, your town will likely have a park or green space that is managed by the local government. Many of these locations will welcome groups to help clean and beautify the park, especially during fall and spring, and may seek volunteers for specific cleanup days and events. Many national parks have family-friendly volunteer opportunities (for example, see https://www.nps.gov/getinvolved for the United States, https://www.pc.gc.ca/en/agence-agency/benevolat-volunteering for Canada, or http://www.nationalparks.gov.uk/about-us/jobs-and-volunteering/volunteering for the United Kingdom). If there are no organized programs like this in your area, create one! You, your family, and some friends can plan a day of caring for the earth and beautifying your community while spending time together having some good clean (or, in this case, dirty) fun. Here are a few suggestions to help this kind of playdate run smoothly:

- Invite families whose children are around the same age.
- Keep an eye on the weather, and dress for it. Remind participants that they will be getting dirty and that it is probably best to wear long pants and closed-toe shoes.

- Bring gloves, garbage bags, and a few rakes, or ask everyone to do so.
- Have each family pack a picnic blanket and lunch, along with equipment for playtime after your cleanup: balls, bubbles, sidewalk chalk, and so on.
- Consider bringing a relevant children's book, such as *Colonel Trash Truck* by Kathleen Crawley, to read before starting the cleanup as a way to engage the children and spark conversation.
- Pick a meeting spot near a small, manageable area of a park or green space. When everyone is gathered and gear is distributed, get to work picking up any trash you see or raking leaves. Set a reasonable time limit for the work so the children don't get restless.
- When you are finished, celebrate your good deed with a picnic lunch and playtime.

 Quick Kindness Tip: When Should We Have Our Cleanup?

A park cleanup is fun any time of year but is particularly meaningful in mid-April, around Earth Day. See chapter 4 for more holiday-related service ideas.

Share, Reflect, and Keep It Going

Whether you complete your kindness project at home or out in your community, a successful playdate with purpose incorporates nearly all of the elements of successful service outlined in the introduction to this book. This kind of playdate is purposeful, simple, and creative and appeals to children and adults of all ages. After the playdate, spend a few moments talking about and reflecting on your experience as you are cleaning up or traveling home. Start by asking a few open-ended questions, such as these:

- How do you think those people felt when you gave them the cards we made?
- How did it make you feel to talk with them?
- Do you think they get a lot of cards and visitors at the senior center? Why or why not?
- Do you have a blanket or stuffed toy that you like to snuggle with or that gives you comfort?
- Do you think the blankets we made today will help those seniors (or children in the hospital) feel warm and snuggly, too?
- Do you have any questions about what we did or saw or about the people we met today?

In these conversations, it's also important to plant the seeds for future efforts.

- What other things could we do another time for this person, this organization, or others?
- Should we follow up with this person or organization later to see how things are going?
- Are there other people in our neighborhood whom we could help? Do you have any ideas about how we might help them?

Quick Kindness Tip: Reflections

If you're not sure how to help your children reflect on their service experiences,

the Doing Good Together website (https://www.doinggoodtogether.org) offers

lists of conversation starters and reflection questions. Tailor the discussion to your

children's levels of maturity and understanding. Don't feel pressure to make any huge

pronouncements about what you've just done as a family. If it was fun and organic, these

kindness activities and volunteering efforts will feel like a normal part of your family

routine, not onetime, big-deal events. Your children might surprise you. One open-ended

comment may bring up other questions and spark a whole different conversation about

issues they'd like to explore or creative ways they might want to give back in the future.

SIMPLE ACTS IN ACTION: SNOW-DAY SERVICE

My family lives in a big apartment building, and my younger daughter, Alaina, is friendly with a neighbor's daughter who is her age. This friendship, cultivated on the bus to summer day camp, has been nurtured through impromptu playdates on rainy Sunday afternoons and on snow days. Over the years, I have used the principles in this chapter to make these get-togethers meaningful as well as fun. Here is one experience that illustrates how simple, enjoyable, and fulfilling these types of playdates can be.

One winter day when the girls were ten, a snow day fell during the week of Valentine's Day. A playdate was soon underway. Together, we read *Somebody Loves You, Mr. Hatch* by Eileen Spinelli, a book about a grumpy elderly man whose life is changed by the discovery of an anonymous valentine in his mailbox. Then the girls baked cookies together and, after sampling their creations, arranged a few small plates of cookies for our building's maintenance staff, who had been working hard all day to clear the adjacent sidewalks of snow. The girls attached little notes of love and gratitude to the top of each plate. They also made a stack of colorful, cheerful valentines for the residents of the assisted-living facility located next door to our building. Later that day, after the snow had stopped, we ventured next door to deliver the valentines to the front-desk staff, who were delighted to receive them. The cards would be distributed on Valentine's Day to any residents whose families lived far away and might not be able to visit.

A snowy afternoon filled with many fun activities—baking, drawing, dancing, sledding, and playing games together—was subtly turned into an afternoon also filled with kindness and generosity. Alaina and her friend had a great day together and finished it with the satisfaction of knowing that they had made others, neighbors as well as strangers, feel loved and appreciated. A win-win.

CHAPTER **TWO**
Planning a Birthday Party with Purpose

"May the kindness you spread keep returning to you."
—Irish blessing

When did children's birthday parties become lavish, hyperthematic events? I think it was sometime after 1969, the year I was born. My birthday is in July, and I was raised in steamy inner-city New Haven, Connecticut. My typical childhood birthday parties included a leaky plastic kiddie pool, a hose, and some sliced watermelon. I thought these parties were the best in the world, but they were not fancy or over-the-top by any stretch of the imagination.

Children's birthday parties today tend to be much more elaborate and focus on a theme or activity of interest to the birthday child, often incorporating themed entertainment, cake, paper products, and goody bags. I've gotten caught up in the madness while hosting parties for my three children over the years. Of course, parents should feel free to celebrate a child's birthday the way they like. However, there are also many ways to blend a little bit of giving into an event that is often so much about getting.

For example, a child's first birthday party provides a particularly special opportunity to serve while you celebrate. At the first-birthday celebration for my older daughter, Emi, she seemed frightened by all the people and noise and nearly fell asleep halfway through the festivities. To be honest, the party was less for her and more for my husband and me, in recognition of having made it through the first exhausting year of parenthood. Since a one-year-old is not fully aware of (and therefore is less invested in) the party activities you've selected or the gifts she has received, hosting a purposeful party for the first birthday is easy and allows you to celebrate your child's milestone—and yours—in a way that sets the tone for a lifetime of generosity.

Service-filled birthday parties can continue well beyond the first birthday. My family has hosted parties with purpose for our children at every age. We've collected baby books at a first-birthday party and pajamas at a first slumber party, created toiletry kits for the homeless at a spa-themed party in the tween years, and collected dog food for the ASPCA the year we adopted our rescue pup. All of these small efforts were quietly integrated into parties filled with all the usual trimmings, adding notes of kindness to already-warm events.

Ultimately, it's all about balance. Every child should feel celebrated on her special day with attention, treats, and gifts to delight her. These moments also provide unique opportunities for children to think about causes and issues they care about, to acknowledge how lucky they are to have special events in their honor, and to empower them to share their birthday joy with others. This chapter suggests ways you can incorporate service into any party, as well as kindness activities and donation opportunities that specifically fit popular party themes.

Adding Kindness to Any Party

Here are a few organizations and websites that can help you add an element of service to any birthday party, no matter its theme.

- The Confetti Foundation (http://confettifoundation.org) supplies birthday-party kits to children who spend their birthdays in the hospital. Kits are donated to participating hospitals across the country. You can host a donation drive at your child's birthday party or purchase the necessary supplies when you are doing your own party shopping. Either way, collect these (new) items:
  - Paper plates, cups, and napkins. Note: All paper goods should be solid colors, stripes, polka dots, or chevron patterns. Don't choose themed paper goods; recipients may not want a particular theme.
  - Baker's twine (all colors)
  - Stickers (in sheets or rolls)
  - White card stock
  - Wooden forks and spoons
  - Tissue-paper medallions, honeycombs, or pompoms (all colors)
  - Birthday-themed books and travel games
  - Crepe-paper streamers
- Family-to-Family (https://www.family-to-family.org) is a grassroots hunger- and poverty-relief organization that connects donors to specific families in need, working to break the cycle of poverty, one family at a time. One of the many programs it sponsors is the Birthday Giving Project, and the project's "birthday party in a box" component is both a collection opportunity and a fun activity for

your child's party. Family-to-Family will help you identify a recipient agency in your community that will ensure that the boxes get into the hands of children who need them.

- Ask guests to donate boxes of cake mix; cans of frosting; birthday candles; children's books; and small, inexpensive toys.
- Children can decorate or wrap shoeboxes (top and bottom separately, so that they can be opened) and can sort the donations into the boxes.
- Children can create colorful, encouraging birthday cards to include in each box.

- The Birthday Party Project (https://www.thebirthdaypartyproject.org) hosts monthly birthday parties at homeless and transitional living facilities across the country. Try shopping the organization's Amazon Wish List (available on the Birthday Party Project's website) for requested party supplies or gifts for the children being served. You can also ask your party guests to bring new toys to donate to the Birthday Party Project in lieu of gifts for the birthday child. After the party, contact the Birthday Party Project to find a location and schedule a time to drop off or mail the gifts. Download a printable thank-you note for your child to use to express gratitude to her guests for supporting the project.

- Pencils of Promise (https://pencilsofpromise.org) is working to make education accessible to underserved children around the world. Children can "Pledge a Birthday" to raise funds for Pencils of Promise, and the website provides a campaign tool kit and social-media images, photographs, and hashtags that can be used for invitations or distributed at the party.

- Gift-sharing websites, such as Echoage (https://www.echoage.com), Share Your Wish (https://shareyourwish.com), and Kids Can Give Too (https://www.kidscangivetoo.com), allow children to give back to charity around their birthdays while still receiving special gifts. Children can register with one of these websites, select a charity to support through a birthday party, and ask guests to make monetary donations in lieu of gifts. These organizations collect the funds and split them between the selected charity and the birthday child, who can purchase a special gift with the money she is given. Evite has also launched a #BirthdayHeroes initiative, with a special line of superhero-themed online invitations that allow children to dedicate their birthday parties to raising money for favorite charities. Guests can donate with a credit card directly through the Evite link (https://www.evite.com/c/evite-birthday-heroes/).

- "Adopt-a-child" websites allow you to purchase gifts for children in need as part of your own celebration:
  - One Simple Wish (https://www.onesimplewish.org) empowers you to spread hope and joy to an individual child affected by foster care, abuse, or neglect. The website is fully interactive, allowing you to search for children by wish category, price range, gender, age range, and location.
  - Daymaker (https://www.daymaker.com) is a child-to-child platform where you can

search a database of children who need help. Your child can select and purchase a specific gift or essential item and can track the item as it is shipped and delivered. This full-circle methodology is unique and creates a more meaningful experience than simply donating toys to a collection drive. The Daymaker website also offers excellent conversation starters to use with your children.

Adding Kindness to a Specific Party Theme

With a little creativity, you can incorporate kindness and generosity into any party theme. For example, it's easy to ask for specific donations to a charity related to your theme in lieu of (or in addition to small) gifts. Of course, requested items need not only relate to the party theme. Hosting a party in late September or early October? Ask guests to bring gently used Halloween costumes to donate to children in foster care. Is your family passionate about helping the hungry in your community? A canned-food collection is a meaningful activity to incorporate into your celebration at any time of year. A December-birthday child might ask for toys to be donated to Toys for Tots or another seasonal toy drive. A summer celebration can collect school supplies to fill backpacks for children in need in your community.

Similarly, no matter what other fun activities you have planned for your child's birthday party, you can always find time for a hands-on kindness project. Sometimes it's helpful to put an activity out on a table as guests are arriving so that children can stay engaged while waiting for the party to start.

A Note About Invitations

A birthday-party invitation, whether paper or electronic, should include information about your child's desire to share the joy of his or her birthday with others. Be sure to describe any donations being requested and any hands-on kindness activities the children might engage in. Provide a description of the mission of the charity being supported (with a website link, if available) and the motivation behind the effort. Consider enhancing the connection with a photograph from the organization's website or a photo of your child engaged in related service. It's important for the guests to understand why these charitable elements are being included in a special celebration and how their gifts, donations, and efforts will make an impact.

Here are a few popular party themes and related suggestions to fill your child's party with kindness and purpose.

Pajama Party or Sleepover

Ask guests to bring a pair of new pajamas, a plush toy, or a blanket for donation to children in need.

Organizations to Work With

- Contact a local social-service agency that helps children who are navigating foster care or living in homeless or domestic-violence shelters. You may also be able to donate pajamas to your local children's hospital or Ronald McDonald House (https://www.rmhc.org), an organization that provides low-cost or free housing and meals to the families of children who are hospitalized far from home.

- Pajama Program (http://pajamaprogram.org) believes that every child deserves a warm and caring nighttime ritual and encourages donation drives to provide pajamas and books to children living in poverty. The website provides all the information and materials you need to host a donation drive. You select an age range and ask guests to bring a new pair of pajamas in that size, along with plush toys and blankets. Pajama Program will provide you with the name and location of a social-service agency in your community that can accept your donations.

- Together We Rise (https://www.togetherwerise.org) provides "sweet cases" (duffel bags filled with essentials, including pajamas, stuffed animals, and blankets) to children in foster care so that they have something besides trash bags to carry their belongings in. You can also register on the website and host a build-a-bike activity or a stuffing party for birthday boxes or sweet cases.

- Similarly, Comfort Cases (https://www.comfortcases.org) assembles filled duffel bags for children entering foster care and is happy to accept donations of new pajamas and new, toddler-safe stuffed animals. Check the website for more information.

- Family-to-Family (https://www.family-to-family.org) coordinates a variety of different programs, including a pajama drive. The website specifically mentions hosting this drive around Valentine's Day to "share the love," but this project can be part of your child's birthday celebration at any time of year. Contact Family-to-Family for help identifying an agency in your area willing to accept your donations.

Hands-On Kindness Projects

- Help children make no-sew fleece blankets (see "Craft No-Sew Fleece Blankets" on page 14 for directions). Blankets can be donated to a nursing home, children's hospital, domestic-violence shelter, or foster-care agency. You may also want to work with Project Linus (www.projectlinus.org), an organization that helps children who are seriously ill, traumatized, or otherwise in need through the gift of a new, handmade blanket or afghan. The Project Linus website gives detailed instructions on how to make a blanket to donate to your local Project Linus chapter. Since its launch in 1999, Project Linus has donated nearly seven million blankets.

- Create "Night Night" packages for Project Night Night (www.projectnightnight.org), which provides childhood essentials to over 25,000 homeless children annually. Every package consists of a tote bag with a children's book, a stuffed animal, and a security blanket. Project Night Night provides detailed information, support, and a how-to video on its website.

- Assemble toiletry kits for a local homeless shelter. Ask guests to bring donations of travel-sized soaps, deodorant, toothpaste, and so on. You can supplement donations by purchasing these items in bulk or at the dollar store. Use quart- or gallon-sized ziplock bags, and ask children to put one of each item in a bag. The children can also create colorful cards to include in each bag.

Sports Party

Ask guests to bring new or gently used sports equipment for donation, particularly equipment that is used in your child's favorite sport.

Organizations to Work With

- Check with your local youth-focused social-service agency (such as the YMCA or YWCA, Big Brothers Big Sisters, or a Special Olympics chapter) to ask whether it accepts donations of new or gently used sports equipment.
- Let's Play It Forward (www.letsplayitforward.org), founded by teenagers, gathers used sports gear and gives it to needy organizations and children.
- Peace Passers (http://peacepassers.org) collects new and used soccer equipment for distribution to communities that don't have access to proper gear.
- Global Sports Foundation (http://globalsportsfoundation.org) provides new and gently used baseball equipment to children around the world.
- Charity Ball (https://charityball.org) provides new soccer balls to poverty-stricken communities worldwide. Your child can start a fund-raising campaign through the website.
- Pitch In For Baseball (https://pifb.org) provides new and gently used baseball and softball equipment to boys and girls around the world who want to play ball but lack equipment. The website offers tons of ways to become involved, including a tool kit and registration for an equipment-donation drive, fund-raising opportunities, and all of the information you need to drop off or ship donations.
- Sports Gift (www.sportsgift.org) is a child-to-child charity that encourages donors to host a "sports gift" party. The website provides information and resources for use at your party, including a list of approved items, T-shirts, banners, and photos of children benefiting from the program. Download a printable label to make shipping your donations easy.
- Goals Haiti (https://www.goalshaiti.org) advances youth leadership through soccer and education in rural Haiti by collecting and donating gently used soccer equipment.
- PeacePlayers (https://www.peaceplayers.org) helps youths from struggling communities by teaching them about peace, leadership, and basketball. You can support the organization's mission with a financial donation or fund-raising drive.
- Speak to the staff at your local sporting-goods store or Play It Again Sports (https://www.playitagainsports.com) location, which may accept donations. For example,

several Play It Again Sports stores in Illinois have partnered with the Sports Shed (https://thesportsshed.org), a nonprofit that provides sports equipment to underresourced children in the Chicago area.

- The One World Play Project (https://www.oneworldplayproject.org) sells colorful, durable soccer balls, and for every purchase, another ball is donated to youth in disadvantaged communities. The balls make great gifts for soccer lovers.

Hands-On Kindness Projects

Lots of sports-themed parties lend themselves to charitable giving through pledges. If you are having a basketball party, for example, consider doing a free-throw challenge. Children can collect pledges from family members to donate a certain amount of money per basket made during the challenge. A bowling party can include a "bowl-a-thon," with pledges made for the number of pins knocked down.

Pool Party

A pool party is the perfect way to celebrate a summer birthday. Whether you are lucky enough to have your own pool or simply host a party at a local facility, your child can share with others the joy and the lifesaving skill of swimming. Ask guests to bring donations of new or gently used swim caps, goggles, and kickboards for local camps.

Organizations to Work With

- A local Special Olympics chapter, YMCA or YWCA, Boys and Girls Club, or other youth organization in your community may accept donated swimming equipment.
- The Elm Project (https://www.elm-project.org) provides a supply list for items you can donate to underresourced summer camps.
- Camp AmeriKids (www.elm-project/camp-amerikids/) is a one-week residential camp program for children who are affected by HIV/AIDS, sickle cell disease, and other chronic illnesses.
- Sunrise Association Day Camps (https://sunrisedaycamp.org) are the only day camps on earth that—at no cost to the participants—exclusively serve young cancer patients and their siblings. With locations in New York, Georgia, Maryland, and Israel, Sunrise encourages fund-raisers in the form of events and walks.
- Goggles for Guppies (www.gogglesforguppies.org) is a distributor of donated swimsuits, caps, and goggles to lifesaving, learn-to-swim programs for at-risk children throughout the world.
- Victory Junction (https://victoryjunction.org/) is a camp located in North Carolina that serves children facing serious health issues, at no cost to their families. They accept both online and mail-in donations.

Hands-On Kindness Projects

If you know your group will have the pool to themselves during the party, plan a "swim-a-thon." Prior to the party, guests can collect pledges from family members for each consecutive lap that they swim without stopping or standing up.

Arts-and-Crafts Party

Whether your child is hosting a party at a pottery-painting shop or you are leaving crayons and paper out to keep little hands busy while you are cutting cake, there are lots of fun options for using art and creativity to help others during a birthday party. Ask guests to bring used or unwanted crayons or new arts-and-crafts materials, such as paint sets, pads of construction paper, crayons, markers, and so on, to donate.

Organizations to Work With

- The Crayon Initiative (http://thecrayoninitiative.org) collects crayons from restaurants, schools, and individuals and recycles them to create brand-new square crayons, which are easier to grasp for children who have special needs or are hospitalized.

- The Dreaming Zebra Foundation (http://dreamingzebra.org) connects community members with disadvantaged children and youth across the country who need art and music resources. It accepts donations of arts-and-crafts materials—fabric, thread, beads, yarn, paints, markers, wooden craft sticks, and so on. If you live in Oregon, you can arrange for your donations to be picked up or ask to be directed to a convenient drop-off location. If you live outside of Oregon, you can ship donations to Dreaming Zebra's headquarters or make a financial donation to further its work. Dreaming Zebra also offers opportunities to sponsor a young artist or purchase items from a wish list.

- Organizations focused on upcycling and redistributing donated art supplies can be found across the United States. Several noteworthy examples include UpCycle Creative Reuse Center (https://www.upcyclecrc.org) in Virginia, Art of Recycle (https://www.artofrecycle.org) in Pennsylvania, and Materials for the Arts (www.nyc.gov/mfta) in New York City. Additionally, your local chapter of the United Way (https://www.unitedway.org) can help you identify an agency in need of donated art supplies.

- Other organizations in your area that may accept donated arts-and-crafts supplies include the Ronald McDonald House (https://www.rmhc.org), children's hospitals, foster-care agencies, or homeless shelters serving families. You might also reach out to public schools serving low-income communities in your area. In these schools, the art curriculum often receives little funding, and many parents cannot afford to provide art supplies for their children. Your children can create cheerful cards of encouragement and support to include with your donations.

Hands-On Kindness Projects

- Paint Stars of Hope (http://starsofhopeusa.org) and donate them to a community that is struggling to recover from tragedy (see "Quick Kindness Tip: Kindness Craft Kits" on page 14).
- The Confetti Foundation (http://confettifoundation.org) supplies party kits to children who spend their birthdays in the hospital. You and your guests can create handmade cards to be placed in the kits. The Confetti Foundation provides some instructions for cards:
  - You need not spend money on actual greeting cards—you can use folded construction paper.
  - Make sure the cards include the message "Happy birthday." If you would like to include other messages, they should be simple, general, positive, and cheerful. Because you do not know recipients' backgrounds or medical conditions, do not include religious messages or phrases such as, "Feel better," or "I hope you go home soon." Some appropriate messages include, "Sending you a smile," or "I hope this card brightens your day."
  - Card makers can sign their first names. Also include your city or state, or both, as the recipients love seeing the different places where people are thinking of them.
  - Use stickers, crayons, or markers. Keep glitter to a minimum.
  - Do not include an envelope.
- Make bracelets or necklaces to exchange or to give to new friends at school. Instructional videos for friendship bracelets can be found online. Children can also make beaded bracelets or necklaces, and you can purchase letter beads so that phrases such as, "You are kind," or "Keep smiling," can be included on each item.

Baking/Cooking/Cupcake-Decorating Party

Request donations of canned goods or nonperishable items for your local food pantry or soup kitchen. Be sure to check with the organization first to find out exactly what types of items are needed and accepted. Or ask guests to donate boxes of cake mix; cans of frosting; birthday candles; children's books; and small, inexpensive toys to create "birthday parties in boxes" for Family-to-Family (see "Adding Kindness to Any Party" on page 23).

Organizations to Work With

- Local food pantries and soup kitchens are typically happy to receive donations. If you do not know the location of your local facility, these websites provide databases that can be searched by zip code:
  - Food Pantries (https://www.foodpantries.org)
  - Feeding America (www.feedingamerica.org/find-your-local-foodbank)
  - Ample Harvest (http://ampleharvest.org/find-pantry/)

- No Kid Hungry (https://www.nokidhungry.org) accepts monetary donations to assist in its mission to alleviate hunger for the more than 13 million American children who live in food-insecure homes.
- Meals on Wheels (https://www.mealsonwheelsamerica.org) programs provide hot meals for homebound clients. Your family can support these programs in a number of ways, including making financial donations, holding fund-raisers, and volunteering to deliver meals.
- Food-recovery organizations—such as Second Harvest (search "Second Harvest" online to find a local chapter), the Food Recovery Network (https://www.foodrecoverynetwork.org), and Feeding America (www.feedingamerica.org)—work to end food waste and feed hungry people in communities across the United States. Try collecting food items from your guests or hosting a cooking party and donating the results to one of these organizations.
- Birthday Cakes 4 Free (http://birthdaycakes4free.com) provides free birthday cakes to financially and socially disadvantaged children and seniors. You can support this work through a financial donation or by volunteering to bake a cake with your party guests. If there is no chapter near you, you can start one!

Hands-On Kindness Projects

- Coordinate an outing with your children (or all of your party guests) to deliver the donations to your local food pantry or soup kitchen. Most likely, the staff will give your group a tour and will talk to the children about food insecurity in your community.
- Create a "giving box" for No Kid Hungry, and place it on a side table at the party. Include a sign asking for spare-change donations and explaining the mission of No Kid Hungry and its impact on childhood hunger in the United States.
- Assemble "birthday parties in boxes" for Family-to-Family (see "Adding Kindness to Any Party" on page 23).
- If the children are baking and decorating cookies or cupcakes, ask them to make an extra batch. Then deliver the treats, along with a note, to a sick or homebound neighbor or to a local homeless shelter or soup kitchen.
- Create snack bags for a local homeless shelter.
  - Children can decorate plain paper lunch bags with markers or stickers. Instruct them to include messages such as, "Enjoy your snack," or "Have a nice day."
  - Purchase a few snack items in bulk, such as individual bags of crackers, chips, or cookies; small boxes of raisins; applesauce cups; and small bottles of water or juice.
  - Create an assembly line and instruct children to fill the bags with one of each item.

Animal-Lover Party

Ask guests to bring chew toys or cans of pet food for donation.

Organizations to Work With

- Your local animal shelter, Humane Society, or ASPCA chapter may accept your guests' donations of food or pet toys, as well as financial contributions.
- The World Wildlife Fund (WWF) (https://www.worldwildlife.org) offers special-occasion fund-raising pages where guests can donate to conservation efforts in lieu of giving gifts. You can also adopt an animal through the WWF and select an animal-themed thank-you gift.
- Heifer International (https://www.heifer.org) works to end poverty and hunger around the world by offering a full range of gift-giving options for holidays and birthdays. Donors can browse the gift catalog and select an amount to donate on behalf of a friend or family member. Each donation amount is used to give an animal to a family in need, providing them with wool, milk, eggs, or other saleable products and increasing the recipients' access to medicine, education, food, and a sustainable livelihood. The donor then selects an honor card that can be printed and mailed or sent electronically to explain the donation to the person in whose honor it was made. Alternatively, you can purchase a gift card by making a donation, and the recipient can redeem the card online to choose her own gift. This type of charitable gift card makes a wonderful alternative goody-bag item for a birthday party.
- Other animal-focused charities that would welcome your financial support include Best Friends Animal Society (https://www.bestfriends.org), Animal Rescue Foundation (https://www.arflife.org), and Canine Companions for Independence (www.cci.org).
- The PetSmart Charities (https://www.petsmartcharities.org) works to facilitate pet adoption and supports animal-welfare organizations. Your local PetSmart location will donate a portion of the proceeds from bags of pet food that are purchased there and may also allow community volunteers to work at adoption events in the store.

Hands-On Kindness Activity

Make pet toys for donation to the ASCPA or your local animal shelter. Here are a few simple ideas:

- Wrap an empty plastic water bottle in a piece of an old T-shirt, and knot or braid the ends. Dogs love the crinkly sound the bottle makes.
- Insert a tennis ball into a colorful old sock, and knot the end.
- Braid several long scraps of fleece into a thick, short rope, and knot both ends.

Superhero, Princess, or Other Character Party

Each year, the trends of popular fictional characters, superheroes, and princesses change, and children often ask for decorations and goody-bag items related to their current favorite characters. Many of these characters demonstrate superpowers or other special skills, and it's fun to incorporate related activities and games—including service projects—into a character-themed party. It may take a bit of creativity to customize a kindness activity to your child's chosen character, but that is part of the fun!

Think about the likes, qualities, or special skills of the party's theme character. If the theme character is a student at a wizard school, for example, ask your child's teacher what school supplies the classroom needs. The teacher will especially appreciate this gesture if your child's birthday falls in the middle of the school year. Request that guests bring those supplies to donate.

If the theme character is a doctor, reach out to your local children's hospital to find out what items they need (books, arts and crafts materials, blankets, toys, and so on), and ask your guests to donate those items. If the theme character is (or loves to dress up as) a princess, ask guests to bring new or gently used dress-up clothes and costume jewelry for donation to a foster-care agency.

Organizations to Work With

Since many superheroes, princesses, and other characters help others, these organizations can fit into any character-themed party:

- Tiny Superheroes (https://tinysuperheroes.com) creates handmade, fully customizable superhero capes. A portion of the proceeds is applied toward the creation of a cape requested by a child battling serious illness or living with a disability. For a thirty-dollar donation, you can provide a completed cape to a child on the waiting list.
- Organizations that provide gift-sharing or "adopt-a-child" opportunities (see "Adding Kindness to Any Party" on page 23) are appropriate for parties focused on characters who help others.
- The Confetti Foundation (http://confettifoundation.org) birthday-card project (see "Arts and Crafts Party" on page 29) is another way to serve like a child's favorite character.
- You can also make cards to send to your local children's hospital or an organization that collects and distributes cards to children battling serious illnesses or facing traumatic experiences through organizations such as Send Kids the World (www.sendkidstheworld.com) and Cards for Hospitalized Kids (www.cardsforhospitalizedkids.com).

Hands-On Kindness Projects

- Sew, iron, or glue patches onto superhero capes, and donate them to children fighting serious illnesses. Simple capes can be precut out of bright fabric or felt, and you can purchase star, heart, thunderbolt, or other design appliqués at a craft store. Children can also draw shapes with fabric paint or markers.
- You can take inspiration from the theme character's superpowers or skills or from causes she supports. For example, if the character fights crime, make thank-you cards and deliver them to your local police station. If the character freezes things, set up a cold-drink station at a local park to provide free refreshment for thirsty joggers.

"Do-Good" Goody Bag Alternatives

Party favors can be expensive, and goody bags full of small toys and candy can seem wasteful. Fortunately, there are other ways to thank your guests for attending.

- Donate to a charity of your choice in honor of all of your guests, and give them each a card explaining the donation. Attach the card to a lollipop to sweeten the deal for young children.
- Rather than giving out entire goody bags, present each guest with a small gift that gives back. Include a card explaining that the gift supports a good cause and why that charity is important to the birthday child, your family, or both. Try shopping for these special party favors at Me to We (https://www.metowe.org), which uses its proceeds to provide health care, water, and other services to underprivileged communities; the St. Jude Gift Shop (https://giftshop.stjude.org), which helps support St. Jude Children's Research Hospital from the proceeds; or one of the organizations listed in "Gifts That Give Back."
- Give each guest a charity gift card so that she can donate to a charity of her choice. TisBest Philanthropy (https://www.tisbest.org) provides a database of more than a million registered charities, so guests are sure to find an organization making a difference on an issue they care about. Global Giving (https://www.globalgiving.org), Heifer International (https://www.heifer.org), Network for Good (https://www.networkforgood.com), and Make a Charity Choice (https://www.charitygiftcertificates.org) provide similar online services.

Gifts That Give Back

Almost everyone loves receiving birthday gifts. Why not give a gift to the birthday child that also supports charities and individuals in need? There are a number of vendors selling high-quality toys, dolls, and games and donating portions of the proceeds to charity. Here are a few examples:

- Cuddle and Kind (https://cuddleandkind.com) sells ethically produced, hand-knit dolls. The sale of each doll provides ten meals for a hungry child.
- Mermaid Pillow Company (https://www.mermaidpillowco.com) sells "mermaid" (also called sequin-back) pillows and has a charitable mission. In its "pillows with purpose" campaign, the company partners with various charities, such as Alex's Lemonade Stand Foundation, Autism Speaks, and Ronald McDonald House, designing special pillows and donating a portion of proceeds to the partner charities.
- Uncommon Goods (https://www.uncommongoods.com) is a sustainable company that is committed to offering employees a living wage (more than twice the US federal minimum) and partners with artists to ensure that products are made from

recycled materials to minimize environmental impact. It donates one dollar to charity for every purchase and offers a variety of gifts, including games and toys.

- Tiny Superheroes (https://tinysuperheroes.com) allows you to fully customize a cape for your child. A portion of the proceeds helps provide a cape to a child with a disability or serious illness.
- Me to We (https://www.metowe.org) sells rafiki bracelets that provide access to clean water and education for children around the world. Each bracelet comes with a code that you can enter on the Me to We website to track the influence of your purchase. Other Me to We items for children include knit hats and finger puppets, all handmade by female artisans in developing countries.
- One World Play (https://www.oneworldplayproject.org) sells durable, colorful soccer balls. For every purchase, another ball is donated to youth in disadvantaged communities.
- St. Jude Children's Research Hospital (https://giftshop.stjude.org) offers a few items for children, including T-shirts and hats.
- UNICEF Market (https://www.market.unicefusa.org) sells cards and gifts that help UNICEF save and protect the world's most vulnerable children.
- WorldCrafts (https://www.worldcrafts.org) develops sustainable, fair-trade businesses among impoverished people around the world. They offer a few items for children, including children's puzzles and finger puppets.
- Change the World by How You Shop (https://www.changetheworldbyhowyoushop.com) is a website that provides an updated listing of "sweatshop-free" toys.
- The World Wildlife Fund's gift center (https://gifts.worldwildlife.org/gift-center/Default.aspx) offers animal-themed gifts in exchange for donations.

Share, Reflect, and Keep It Going

Having hosted nearly forty birthday parties (and counting) for my three children over the years, I fully appreciate how exhausting and hectic party days can be. It is hard enough to remember all the many details (candles? cake knife? napkins?), snap a few photographs, and make sure that everyone is happy and well fed. Incorporating kindness and service may feel like just one more thing to remember. But with a little advance planning, a purposeful party is possible and worthwhile. It incorporates many of the keys to a successful family service project—purpose, creativity, simplicity—and they are all focused on and driven by the interests of your child. Most importantly, your child's actions will make an impression on all of the children and adults in attendance. The ripple effects of goodness from this one day are limitless.

Once the guests have departed, help all your children (regardless of whose birthday it is) process the experience by reflecting with questions like these:

- What was your favorite part of the party?
- Did you see all of the items we collected (or created)? How many did we have in all?
- How did it make you feel to share your birthday celebration with people who are in need?
- Do you think the children who attended and donated feel good about being here today and learning about the charity you are supporting?
- What can we do now, after the party, to continue supporting that charity? Should we send them some photos from your party along with the donations?
- When we write your thank-you notes to your friends, should we follow up with them and tell them about the many ways their generosity will help others?

SIMPLE ACTS IN ACTION: A CAUTIONARY TALE

If your child invites a large number of guests to her birthday party, a pile of new and sometimes duplicate toys will inevitably be given as gifts, adding to the seemingly endless clutter in a young family's home. It may seem both logical and charitable to make room for the new toys by donating duplicate gifts or older toys that the child no longer enjoys. I have often struggled with this issue, and I learned valuable lessons in one particular attempt to come up with a solution.

When my younger daughter, Alaina, was five years old, my friend Jenna and I decided to embark on a birthday giving project for a local charity. Jenna's son was the same age as Alaina, and we mothers had been commiserating over the underappreciated, duplicate gifts that our children received on their birthdays. We vowed to work with our children to help them appreciate their good fortune and learn to share their abundance of toys with children who might not have any. Jenna and I arranged to bring our children to visit an after-school enrichment program in an underresourced public school, and we offered to bring some donated toys so that each student who had a birthday during the school year could receive a gift.

After we had spent a pleasant hour playing and drawing with the children in the program, Alaina and Jenna's son were asked to pass out the toys we had brought to donate. Disaster ensued. There were tears all around: our children were overwhelmed by having to give up their treasures, and the other children scuffled over the toys.

In retrospect, I realized what Jenna and I had done wrong. It had been unreasonable to expect five-year-olds to understand what we were doing or to want to share their toys. Also, Jenna and I should have been more sensitive to the discomfort caused by having our children hand out the toys to the children in the program, an action that set up an awkward power dynamic between the two groups. The good intentions of this teachable moment had been lost. I learned that I could encourage my children to be grateful for all they had *and* ask them to consider sharing some of their abundance, but I needed to give them control over how, when, and what to give.

You know your children best and can decide if and when to suggest donating some toys or requesting donations in lieu of gifts. I've provided a variety of ideas in this chapter to match many maturity levels and interests. The goal is always to make everyone feel good—the birthday child as well as the party guests—and to engage the birthday child in the planning and execution as much as possible so that she understands and feels proud of her actions.

CHAPTER **THREE**
Milestones with Meaning

"How beautiful a day can be when kindness touches it."
— George Elliston, American journalist

As we go about our daily routines, we can always find ways to be kind to others. However, there are days that merit special attention because they mark milestones in the lives of children. Many people honor these significant occasions by inviting loved ones to participate in or witness special events, taking and sharing photographs, giving speeches or writing letters to the child, or hosting festive celebrations filled with food, decorations, and gifts.

As children get older, there are more opportunities for this kind of public celebration. Sweet sixteens, school graduations, quinceañeras, religious confirmations, and bar or bat mitzvah celebrations are just a few of the rites of passage in the preteen and teen years, and many of these celebrations are marked by the guest of honor giving back in some way. For example, for her bat mitzvah celebration, my daughter Emi asked for donations in lieu of gifts and raised money for a homeless women's and children's shelter in New Orleans. At her party, instead of offering bags of candy as guests departed, we gave out sweets made by a bakery that donates a portion of the proceeds to charity.

But what if your children are young and these types of celebrations are years away? Never fear! For a family with young children, there are many moments—large and small—that commemorate important life events. The birth of a new baby; a christening, bris, or naming ceremony; the first day of school; the first lost tooth; and many more are all moments to be recognized. Some of these events merit a celebration with guests, while others are marked quietly at home, but each one is worthy of being acknowledged.

Incorporating a small act of kindness is a way of sharing your joy and sense of accomplishment with those who are less fortunate, and it enhances your family's gratitude for the special moment you are experiencing.

Serving at Any Celebration

Many milestones involve special celebrations with family and friends. Sadly, when everyone goes home, the leftover food and decorations often end up in the trash. However, with a little advance planning, these items don't have to go to waste. Try one of these options to put your excess treats and decorations to good use.

Food

If there are trays of food that have not been opened, they may be donated to a food-rescue organization such as Second Harvest or its affiliate in your community. If you are not familiar with your local food-rescue organizations, there are several national databases that can be searched by zip code, including Sustainable America (https://sustainableamerica.org/foodrescue) and Food Rescue US (https://foodrescue.us). Trays of untouched food can also be delivered to a local church or homeless shelter or given to the staff of the party venue.

Flowers

Even a single event, gala, wedding, or other special celebration can generate hundreds of pounds of floral waste. Rather than discarding the floral arrangements, consider rearranging the flowers and delivering them to a local nursing home, assisted-living center, or hospital.

Celebrating a New Baby with Service

There are many ways to add thoughtful touches to the celebration of a new member of your family.

Plant a Tree

Whether you are planning a special celebration with family and friends or are quietly settling into home life with your new baby, you can memorialize this special time by planting a tree. This small gesture helps the planet and gives you an opportunity to talk to your family about our collective responsibility to care for the earth. You can plant a sapling in your own yard or request to plant one in a green space in your town. If you live in the United States and are unsure what kind of tree will thrive in your climate, there is an excellent resource on the Arbor Day website (https://www.arborday.org/trees). Click on "Shop Our Tree Nursery," then click on "Best Tree Finder." Enter your zip code, and click the types of trees you are interested in, such as amount of shade, height, and so on.

If you are not able to plant a tree yourself, you can donate to one of these organizations, which will then plant a tree in honor of your new baby or any other special occasion:

- One Tree Planted (https://onetreeplanted.org)
- The National Forest Foundation (https://www.nationalforests.org)
- A Living Tribute (https://www.alivingtribute.org)
- Earth Day Network's Reforestation Project (https://www.earthday.org)
- Arbor Day Foundation (https://www.arborday.org)
- The Jewish National Fund (http://usa.jnf.org/jnf-tree-planting-center/)

Incorporate Service into a Baby Shower

Family members and friends often hold a party to help parents prepare for a new arrival, creating many opportunities for service. If you choose to ask guests for charitable donations in lieu of gifts, be sure your invitation includes information about the charity you are supporting. During the celebration itself, prominently display a framed message about your charitable giving or activity, or put the message on signs or cards at each table. You may want to follow up with your guests afterward, thanking them for their support and describing how many items were collected or how much money was donated so that they feel connected to the effort. Here are some meaningful donation items to consider requesting.

Diapers and Wipes

Diaper need is a significant problem in the United States. According to the National Diaper Bank Network (http://nationaldiaperbanknetwork.org), one in three families in America struggles to afford diapers. Even government safety-net programs do not cover the costs of diapers or personal-care items. The monthly cost of diapers is very high, forcing some families to leave the same diaper on a baby for an entire day, creating health risks and emotional problems. Consider collecting diapers of any size at your celebration. The National Diaper Bank Network, The Good+Foundation (https://goodplusfoundation.org), or Baby2Baby (http://baby2baby.org) can help you identify a social-service organization in your community to which you can deliver your donations.

Children's Books

Researchers Nicole Alston-Able and Virginia Berninger have found that reading and writing with young children lays the foundations for long-term success in school and work. Collecting and donating books is a powerful way to give back to children in your community, and piles of colorful children's books can add to the festive décor of a baby shower or birth celebration. Many nonprofits and underresourced public-school classrooms in your community need children's books and would welcome donations. To find homes for your donations, you can reach out to local social-service agencies, homeless and domestic-violence shelters, children's hospitals, the Ronald McDonald House (https://www.rmhc.org), literacy programs, foster-care agencies, or your country's department or ministry of education. If you'd like to support national and international organizations that collect books, explore these websites:

- Better World Books (https://www.betterworldbooks.com)
- Books for Africa (https://www.booksforafrica.org)
- DonationTown (http://donationtown.org)
- Promising Pages (https://promisingpages.org)

Infant and Toddler Pajamas

Pajama Program (http://pajamaprogram.org) and Family-to-Family (https://www.family-to-family.org) can provide you with the names and locations of social-service agencies in your community that can accept donations of pajamas.

Stuffed Animals or Plush Toys

It is sometimes difficult to find organizations that will accept stuffed animals, as health and cleanliness concerns often prevent donated plush toys from being distributed to children in need. However, first responders in your community might accept these donations, as police, firefighters, and emergency medical technicians (EMTs) often keep stuffed animals on hand to offer to the traumatized children they encounter in emergencies. A nonprofit called Stuffed Animals for Emergencies (https://stuffedanimalsforemergencies.org) was established for this purpose. Other organizations such as domestic-violence or homeless women's shelters, foster-care agencies, and other social-service agencies that assist displaced, traumatized, abused, or homeless children might accept donated stuffed toys as well.

Create Dual-Purpose Decorations

Instead of buying costly flowers, consider creating table centerpieces and other decorations out of colorful baby items that can be donated to local charities after the event.

- Create a "diaper cake." After the event, donate the diapers to a homeless shelter serving families, a domestic-violence shelter serving women and children, or a foster-care agency. Here are instructions to make a simple diaper cake:
  - Roll up a size 1 diaper (cloth or disposable), and secure it with a rubber band. Repeat until you have 20 rolled-up diapers.
  - Arrange the diapers around a long, skinny object, such as a champagne bottle, a tall bottle of baby shampoo, or even a paper-towel tube, and secure them with a large rubber band.
  - If desired, roll up more diapers to create additional tiers for the "cake."
  - Cover the rubber bands with decorative ribbon. Keep embellishments to a minimum so that the cakes can be easily disassembled and the diapers donated after the party.
- Stack colorful board books and arrange them in the center of a table. You can donate them to your local children's hospital, Ronald McDonald House (https://www.rmhc.org), library, or foster-care agency.

- Fill mason jars with crayons, and donate them to the Crayon Initiative (https://thecrayoninitiative.org).
- Build a pyramid of small stuffed animals or rolled-up burp cloths tied with colorful ribbon, and donate them to a social-service agency that helps families living in poverty, or give them to your local firehouse for use by first responders.
- Fill clear bowls or plastic boxes with child-sized soccer balls, and donate them to the Big Brothers Big Sisters program or a YMCA, YWCA, or other summer-camp program.
- Arrange colorful toys, such as trucks, shape sorters, or blocks, in the center of each table. Try to keep sets together so that they can be reassembled and donated more easily. Give them to Toys for Tots, a foster-care agency, or to any organization serving homeless or poverty-stricken families.

Serve Sweet Treats That Give Back

All of these desserts, which can also be included in goody bags for guests, can be shipped, and the retailers donate a portion of the proceeds to charity.

- Treat House (https://treathouse.com) makes gourmet crispy rice treats and donates a portion of the proceeds to the Leukemia and Lymphoma Society.
- Give (www.thecookiethatgives.com) uses ingredients sourced from fair-trade farmers to make their cookies. These cookies can be purchased in bulk, and 15 percent of the proceeds are donated to a charity that you select from the company's list.
- Cookies for Kids' Cancer (www.cookiesforkidscancer.org) creates gourmet cookies with ten different flavor options. Every box sold supports research at America's leading pediatric cancer centers.
- Cheryl's Cookies (https://www.cheryls.com/charitable-gifts) runs the Baking Life Better program. Every purchase supports nine national charities as well as more than a dozen local nonprofits in central Ohio.

 Quick Kindness Tip: Religious and Cultural Milestones

All of these ideas—and more—can be incorporated into ceremonies or celebrations for religious or cultural milestones, such as Aqiqah (a sacrifice to celebrate a birth) in Islam, Mundan (haircutting) and Karnavedha (ear piercing) in Hinduism, *upsherin* (a boy's first haircut) in Judaism, and so on. The most important thing is to view each of these moments as opportunities to express gratitude for your own blessings by sharing your joy and abundance with others.

Celebrating Everyday Milestones with Service

Those little events that tug at your heart, make you well up with tears, and prompt you to grab your phone to capture a photo—you can spread your joy through service in those moments, too.

First Steps

Honor the exciting day your child takes his first steps with a donation to Soles4Souls (https://soles4souls.org), a national nonprofit that creates sustainable jobs and provides poverty relief through the distribution of shoes worldwide. Better still, sort through your closets and create a pile of gently used shoes to donate. The Soles4Souls website gives detailed instructions on how to drop off or ship donations.

First Haircut

The first trip to the barbershop or hair salon is often a day filled with tears, photos, and lollipops. Consider donating to St. Baldrick's (https://www.stbaldricks.org), an organization that has raised more than $232 million dollars since 2005, primarily through events where volunteers agree to shave their heads in solidarity with (and to raise funds for) children with cancer. There are many wonderful organizations that support children struggling with illness, but St. Baldrick's has a particular focus on hair, making it a perfect fit for a child's first haircut.

First Word

Whether it is your first child or your fourth, hearing the first babbled word (or what resembles an actual word) is a milestone that is greeted with wonder and tremendous joy. Consider honoring this special moment with a donation to an organization helping families who may never have the privilege of hearing the sweet sounds of their babies' voices. The American Society for Deaf Children (http://deafchildren.org) provides membership, American Sign Language education, provider directories, and support to families with children who are deaf.

Giving Up a Pacifier, Blanket, or Stuffed Toy

If your child has a special "lovie," plush toy, or blanket or is attached to a pacifier at bedtime, the day he lets it go is a big deal. Incorporating a service project that helps other children feel safe and loved might provide motivation and comfort to your child during what can be a difficult transition. Consider making a financial donation to Project Linus (www.projectlinus.org) or working with your children to create simple fleece blankets to donate to your local chapter (see "Pajama Party or Sleepover" on page 25).

Completion of Toilet Training

While this milestone is more of a process than a onetime event, the end of toilet training provides an opportunity to support families struggling with diaper needs.

When all is said and done, you will likely have packages of unopened diapers, training pants, and wipes at home. Consider supplementing these with a few new packages and donating them to a social-service agency that supports families living in poverty in your community. If you can't identify an agency near you, the National Diaper Bank Network (http://nationaldiaperbanknetwork.org) can help you find one.

First Lost Tooth

Often when a child loses a tooth for the first time, a big deal is made about the Tooth Fairy. Notes are written, coins are left under pillows, and some families read a thematic bedtime story or use a special pillow to hold the lost tooth. To mark this exciting moment, consider taking your child to buy toothbrushes and toothpaste to donate to a local homeless shelter or food pantry. In my experience with these organizations, oral-hygiene products are some of the most in-demand personal-care items, and donations run out quickly. Another wonderful charity to support on this happy occasion is Operation Smile (https://www.operationsmile.org), which brings life-changing treatment to children around the world who are suffering from cleft lip and cleft palate.

 Quick Kindness Tip: Special Lost-Tooth Timing

If your child loses a tooth in February, you have a special opportunity to make a connection to National Children's Dental Health Month. Try donating toothbrushes and toothpaste to children in need. See chapter 4 for more ways to celebrate National Children's Dental Health Month and other events on the calendar.

First Day of School

Whether your child is starting nursery school or kindergarten, the milestone of embarking on a lifelong journey of learning is a perfect time to remind children how lucky they are to be able to go to school at all. Back-to-school season is full of opportunities to make a difference in the lives of children living in poverty, who may not have the resources they need to start school with confidence and dignity. My family always participates in Operation Backpack, sponsored by Volunteers of America (https://www.voa.org/operation-backpack), at this time of year. We combine shopping for our own school supplies with purchasing items to help fill backpacks for children in our community. More information about this project can be found in "Service Ideas for Summer" in chapter 7.

Learning to Ride a Bike

The day your child finally masters riding a bike without training wheels or assistance from an adult is a thrilling day. After all the scraped knees and elbows, the exhilaration of finally "getting it" is a moment worth celebrating. It also provides an excellent opportunity for your child to share his joy with a child who might not be lucky enough to have a bike or a parent from whom to learn to ride.

- Together We Rise (https://www.togetherwerise.org) supports children in foster care. You can register on its website to host a build-a-bike event with family and friends (see "Pajama Party or Sleepover" on page 25).

- The 88Bikes Foundation (www.88bikes.org) provides bikes to girls around the world, including girls who have been affected by human trafficking. The 88Bikes Foundation partners with vetted, locally-run nongovernmental organizations, purchases bikes from local vendors (supporting the local economy), hires local labor to assemble and deliver the bikes, and connects each recipient one-to-one with her donor. You can send an email with a photo of your family, and you will receive a personal confirmation within a few days. You are then assigned a bike number. Within three to six months, you will receive a photo of the girl to whom your bike was donated. This is a tangible way for your child to connect to the recipient of his generosity.

- Trips for Kids (https://www.tripsforkids.org) is a nonprofit that provides cycling experiences through a network of chapters around the United States to promote a healthy, recreational lifestyle. The organization offers a trail-rides program, an earn-a-bike workshop, and mobile bike clinics. It also advocates for bike recycling.

- A quick online search for your area will likely uncover a bike-recycling organization or other charity that provides bikes to local children. For example, Bikes for Kids CT (https://www.bikesforkidsct.org) supports children in Connecticut but partners with nonprofits around the world to provide bikes for children in need. The Bikes for Kids Foundation (www.bikesforkidsfoundation.org) operates in Colorado, and Recycle Bikes for Kids (www.recyclebikesforkids.org) is located in Arkansas.

Moving Up to the Next Grade

The last few days of school are bittersweet for young children—saying goodbye to beloved teachers and friends, cleaning out cubbies and desks, and carrying home heavy bags of classwork and art. As parents, we feel terrible throwing any of our children's art away, but realistically, keeping and storing everything is impractical. One solution is to sort through drawings, select a few favorites to save, and then donate the rest to a local nursing home or children's hospital or turn them into notes of gratitude and encouragement for soldiers. These notes can be sent to one of the many organizations supporting soldiers and their families, including Operation Gratitude (https://www.operationgratitude.com) and Operation Help a Hero (https://www.operationhelpahero.org). You can also bundle up colorful artwork and send it to Color A Smile (https://colorasmileorg.presencehost.net/), a nonprofit that delivers artwork to senior citizens, soldiers, those battling serious illnesses, or anyone in need of a smile.

Share, Reflect, and Keep It Going

There is perhaps no better time to consider giving back than while we are celebrating a joyful moment as a family. Regardless of our circumstances or the struggles we may face in our daily lives, these special times provide an opportunity for reflection as we are filled with wonder, gratitude, and the desire to share good feelings with others. Finding a purpose in the midst of our joy should be easy, and acknowledging it with a simple gesture is entirely appropriate. Planning milestone celebrations with meaning has particular intergenerational appeal, as adults in your family will see the value of taking advantage of this fleeting, pure moment of joy. I know that as I get older, I am constantly reminded that happy memories are to be cherished and are enhanced by sharing with others.

Here are some reflection questions to consider not only with your children but also with your spouse, partner, or extended family as you celebrate milestones through service:

- What does this moment mean to our family? How have we honored it by doing something kind for another person?
- What do we actually need for this event (or baby)? How can we redirect some of our abundance to others who are in need?
- How did you feel today as you lost your first tooth, rode your bike for the first time, headed off for your first day of school, or celebrated some other milestone? How can we make other people feel all the wonderful things you are feeling (proud, happy, excited, and so on)?
- What can we do to continue to help this person or charity in the months and years ahead?

SIMPLE ACTS IN ACTION: GROWING TREES AND GROWING CHILDREN

As we look out over a landscape of uncertainty about the future of our planet and environment, it seems to me that the most concrete way to make a small but tangible difference is to plant a tree. I've been planting trees in honor of friends' and family members' milestones for many years, typically through the Jewish National Fund (JNF). This organization plants trees in Israel and sends a beautiful certificate to each person being honored. One of my favorite opportunities to give the gift of a tree is the celebration a new baby. There is wonderful symbolism and symmetry in planting a tree in honor of a new life. As the child grows, the family will know that a tree grows in parallel, replenishing the earth in small but significant ways. When a neighbor recently invited me to a naming ceremony for her newborn son, I was excited to buy the baby a little outfit, and I also donated to the JNF to plant a tree in his name. The JNF certificate is a beautiful gift all by itself, and the donation was deeply appreciated, as the mother expressed how this gift would be remembered long after clothing and toys were outgrown and discarded.

As children grow older, they learn to appreciate the significance of these types of gifts. For example, my family recently donated to the JNF to plant several trees for a friend's son, who was celebrating his bar mitzvah in Israel with his extended family. While the son was unable to see the new trees during that trip, his thank-you note to us read, "It means so much to me for you guys to plant trees in honor of my life. Thank you so much. I hope to see the trees the next time I go to Israel." There's no better feeling than giving a child (or anyone) a gift that is meaningful and genuinely appreciated.

CHAPTER **FOUR**
Kindness Month by Month

"Service to others is the rent you pay for your room here on earth."
—Muhammad Ali, American boxer, activist, and philanthropist

I believe that every family can find time for at least one good deed each month. It's not an unrealistic goal. With intentionality and an open heart, you can always find time to cultivate kindness and actively engage in service with children. At the end of each month, sit for a moment with your family, and take a look at the new month ahead. The opportunities will appear if you are looking for them.

In my family, there is a seven-year age gap between the oldest and the youngest child. There are times when we can all participate in a service project together (particularly around the end-of-year holidays), but at other times, we might need to split up to find the right opportunity for each child. For example, my oldest child, Emi, celebrates her birthday in February. She often hosts a party with purpose for her friends, incorporating a service activity or fund-raiser benefiting a favorite charity. Around the same time, I encourage my youngest child, Alaina, and her friends to create valentines for soldiers, which we send to Soldiers' Angels (see "February 14: Valentine's Day" on page 49). My middle child, Archie, and I might sort through gently used coats, hats, gloves, and scarves to donate to Goodwill (www.goodwill.org), the New York Cares annual coat drive, or a local agency collecting warm gear for the homeless. In February—and every month—we let special occasions, holidays, and weather guide our efforts, and we try to find a way for everyone in the family to participate in an age-appropriate way.

Service Ideas for Each Month

The calendar is so busy, especially for young families, that it may seem impossible to fit service into your routine. But you *can* do it. Developing a habit of service takes practice and persistence. Stay open to the possibilities that the calendar presents.

What follows is an extensive listing of monthly service opportunities, but it is by no means exhaustive. Your culture, family, faith, school, and community will guide you to other holidays, special occasions, commemorations, and milestones when you and your children can find time to incorporate service and acts of kindness into your busy lives. This calendar includes many American holidays but also acknowledges similar events in other parts of the world that can be honored by using many of the same ideas.

January

January 1: New Year's Day and World Day of Peace

Similar events: Oshogatsu (Japan, January 1), Chinese New Year (dates vary), Seollal (Korea, dates vary), Tet (Vietnam, dates vary), International Day of Peace (September 21)

The first day of a new year is a perfect time to recommit your family to doing more service. At this time of year, many families are finishing up holidays during which children have been showered with gifts and joyful experiences, so this is a great time to turn your family's focus outward again. Make a list of service-related resolutions, or create a family kindness challenge for the new year ahead.

In honor of the World Day of Peace, consider creating and sharing peace-themed arts-and-crafts projects. Begin by reading a book together, such as *The Children's Peace Book* by Jolene DeLisa, *Grandfather Gandhi* by Arun Gandhi and Bethany Hegedus, or *The Story of Ferdinand* by Munro Leaf. Talk with your children about the definitions of *peace* and *conflict resolution* within the context of your own family. Give each child a sheet of paper and markers, and ask the children to answer the question, "What does peace look like?" in words and illustrations. Collect small, smooth rocks (or purchase some at a craft store in advance), and paint colorful peace signs on each one. Take a walk around your neighborhood and leave the rocks for others to find. Help your children use sidewalk chalk to share messages of hope and peace with illustrations of doves, rainbows, and peace signs, and include messages such as, "Peace on Earth," or "Peace begins with a smile."

Third Monday in January: Martin Luther King Jr. Day of Service

Similar event: Nelson Mandela International Day (July 18)

In the United States, this holiday honors the life and legacy of civil-rights leader Dr. Martin Luther King Jr. Rather than seeing this event as just a day off from school and work, the Points of Light Foundation (https://ww2.pointsoflight.org/mlkday), the

Corporation for National and Community Service (https://www.nationalservice.gov/mlkday), and other nonprofit organizations encourage Americans to give back to their communities in honor of Dr. King's legacy. If you live outside the United States, these websites can provide ideas for ways to give back in your own community to honor your country's civil-rights leaders.

January 24: Compliment Day

Sincere compliments are a beautifully simple act of kindness, and even young children can learn to give them. Challenge each other to give a unique compliment to each person you see today.

February

Black History Month

Similar event: Day of Respect for Cultural Diversity (Argentina, second Monday in October)

Black History Month is observed in February in the United States and Canada and in October in the United Kingdom, to honor the contributions to society made by people of African heritage. Many civic and community organizations, children's museums, and schools offer service opportunities and celebratory events during Black History Month. For more ideas, see www.africanamericanhistorymonth.gov.

National Children's Dental Health Month

We often take for granted the availability of simple dental-hygiene tools such as toothbrushes, toothpaste, and mouthwash, but for many families living in poverty, personal-care items are luxuries and are not covered by government assistance. Consider taking children to the store and purchasing toothbrushes and toothpaste to donate to social-service agencies serving homeless children or those living in foster care. If you are also creating valentines for these organizations, you can attach a small bag containing a travel-sized toothbrush and tube of toothpaste to each card.

February 14: Valentine's Day

There's no better time to spread love than Valentine's Day. Children can make cards to donate in your local community or through national organizations such as Soldiers' Angels (https://soldiersangels.org), which sponsors the Valentines for Veterans campaign. Another option is to write a "love letter" to a stranger. An organization called The World Needs More Love Letters (www.moreloveletters.com) requests nominations of people who need encouragement and love, and posts selected names on its website. You can help your children compose short letters to some of these individuals and send the letters directly to those people through addresses provided by the organization.

February 17: Random Acts of Kindness Day

The Random Acts of Kindness Foundation (https://www.randomactsofkindness.org) believes in spreading kindness through schools, communities, and homes. Visit the website for information, resources, and inspiration.

Third Monday in February: Presidents Day

Similar events: Benito Juárez's birthday (Mexico, third Monday in March), Mahatma Gandhi's birthday (India, October 2), Bonifacio Day (Philippines, November 30), and the Emperor's Birthday (Japan, date varies)

Presidents Day honors all presidents of the United States. It is a federal holiday and typically a day off from school, creating some time and space for conversation and service with children. Use the day as an opportunity to discuss issues of civics, government, leadership, and democracy and to engage in advocacy together as you explore participatory government. You and your children can research issues of concern in your community or nation. Then, reach out to your elected officials via emails or handwritten letters to express your opinions, or you can find online petitions that the adults in your family can sign.

As this holiday falls during the winter in the Northern Hemisphere, it also provides a good opportunity to use the time off to sort through gently used clothing and outerwear to donate to charity. Your local Goodwill (www.goodwill.org) or Salvation Army Family Store (https://satruck.org) is always willing to accept such donations.

March

National Reading Month and Read Across America Day (March 2)

These events (http://www.nea.org/grants/886.htm) celebrate books and encourage support of local libraries and schools. Spring is also a good time to sort through your home library and donate gently used books to children in your community or to an organization such as Better World Books (https://www.betterworldbooks.com), Books for Africa (https://www.booksforafrica.org), or Promising Pages (https://promisingpages.org).

March 17: Saint Patrick's Day

This holiday is a fun time to celebrate Irish heritage by engaging children in arts-and-crafts activities focused on luck, kindness, and gratitude. For example, try the Kindness Clovers activity, created by Deanna Hershberger for Artsy Momma (https://artsymomma.com/kindness-clovers-printable-activity.html). Each kindness clover includes a phrase such as, "You are a great friend," or "I'm lucky to have you." Blank clovers can be used to write personal messages of love and gratitude. Give decorated clovers to family members, friends, teachers, and coaches. Children can also create rainbow drawings or collages using colored paper or markers, and they can use the pot of gold at the end of the rainbow to write all of the ways they feel lucky in their lives. Families can bake colorful shamrock or rainbow cookies and deliver them, along with notes or kindness clovers, to a nursing home, an assisted-living center, or an ill or elderly neighbor.

March 20: International Day of Happiness

Established by the United Nations, this celebration (www.dayofhappiness.net) acknowledges how important it is for people around the world to be happy, with the goals of seeking to end poverty, reduce inequality, and protect our planet. Expressing our love and care for others is one of the easiest ways to spread happiness on this day. Children can be encouraged to call a faraway relative or friend who might be lonely, or you can leave flowers on the doorstep of a neighbor who is ill or grieving. Children can create simple notes with loving messages such as, "Your friendship makes me happy," or "I have so many happy memories with you," and share them with family, friends, and classmates. If you and your family would like to tackle more global issues of happiness, you can explore the Day of Happiness website for ideas on life-changing local actions that make a difference in your community or for ways to help children be happier and more resilient.

April

Volunteer Appreciation Month and National Volunteer Week (third week of April)

Volunteer Appreciation Month and National Volunteer Week are opportunities to celebrate service and recognize volunteers. The Points of Light Foundation website (https://ww2.pointsoflight.org/nvw) provides more information and a searchable database of volunteer opportunities.

Good Deeds Day (date varies)

Good Deeds Day (www.good-deeds-day.org) seeks to bring individuals together around the world to perform acts of kindness and service for other people and for the planet. Sign up online to find ideas, resources, and tips and to download materials.

Arbor Day (date varies)

The date for this holiday varies according to the climate of each country or area, but it generally occurs in the spring. Arbor Day (https://www.arborday.org) is centered on trees and is a perfect time for families to get outside and volunteer together. The best way to celebrate Arbor Day is to plant a tree or donate to one of the many organizations that plant trees around the world (see "Celebrating a New Baby with Service" on page 39).

April 22: Earth Day

Earth Day is a key part of the worldwide environmental movement, and in my experience, it is one of the most popular days for volunteering in spring. Many parks and nonprofit foundations sponsor events around Earth Day, and the Earth Day Network (https://www.earthday.org) maintains an excellent website filled with resources. Can't find a family-friendly Earth Day event in your area? Create one. Organize a park cleanup with friends, plant a tree in your yard, or create a plastic-bottle donation and recycling drive in your apartment building.

Wednesday of the Last Full Week of April: Administrative Professionals Day

Administrative Professionals Day honors the many helpers in your family's world: assistants, secretaries, receptionists, and so on. Parents who work outside of the home rely on administrative professionals on a daily basis and often speak fondly of those individuals at home. Likewise, every school, daycare center, camp, and after-school activity is powered by administrative staff who keep those organizations running smoothly. Encourage children to thank the administrative professionals in their lives. Simple notes of kindness, along with real or paper flowers, plates of homemade cookies, or colorful handprint paintings (because administrative professionals always give a helping hand) can be left on desks for a sweet surprise.

May

Military Appreciation Month

Regardless of your family's personal connection to the military, it's important for children to understand and respect the sacrifices made by men and women who serve in the armed forces. Operation We Are Here (www.operationwearehere.com) is a website that provides a comprehensive listing of all organizations that accept cards, care packages, and other donations for active-duty military, veterans, and military families. Try working with one of these organizations to help your children show gratitude for those who keep us safe:

- Operation Gratitude (https://www.operationgratitude.com)
- Operation Care Package (www.operationcarepackages.org)
- Operation Paperback (www.operationpaperback.org)
- Soldiers' Angels (https://soldiersangels.org)
- Support Our Troops (https://www.supportourtroops.org)
- Any Soldier (www.anysoldier.com)
- Operation Shoebox (https://www.operationshoebox.com)
- Books for Soldiers (http://booksforsoldiers.com)
- Stack Up (https://stackup.org)
- Operation Help a Hero (https://www.operationhelpahero.org)
- Operation Homefront (https://www.operationhomefront.org)

First full week in May: Teacher Appreciation Week and National Teacher Day (that Tuesday)

Most schools, whether public or private, will sponsor activities around Teacher Appreciation Week. Schools may ask parents to refrain from giving individual gifts so that all faculty and staff are thanked consistently and appropriately, but there are other ways to help your children show gratitude to their teachers. Personal, handwritten cards or drawings are always deeply appreciated. Don't forget the other special folks who help to make a school safe, clean, and joyful: librarians, security staff, cafeteria workers, office staff, maintenance staff, crossing guards, and so on.

Mother's Day (date varies)

In the United States, this holiday is celebrated on the second Sunday in May, but mothers are celebrated the world over. Take this special day to show love and appreciation for the mothers, grandmothers, aunts, cousins, caregivers, and other special women in your children's lives. Despite what the media and advertisers would suggest, expensive gifts, lavish flower arrangements, and complicated meals are not necessary to express love to motherly figures. In my experience, every person being acknowledged on this day most appreciates simple gestures, such as a kind word of gratitude, a hug, a homemade card with sincere sentiments, a simple meal, or an opportunity to relax a bit and enjoy family time together.

Combining a celebration of Mom with service in the community, making family memories and creating new traditions along the way, is another way to make the day special. A kindness activity you can do at home is creating small toiletry kits of travel-sized soap, deodorant, shampoo, toothpaste, dental floss, and toothbrushes, along with feminine-hygiene products, soft socks, and a few luxury items, such as lipstick or perfume. You can deliver these kits to a domestic-violence or women's shelter in your community, where they will be deeply appreciated.

Last Monday in May: Memorial Day

Similar events: Anzac Day (Australia, April 25), Remembrance Day (November 11), and National Heroes' Day (Philippines, last Monday in August)

Memorial Day is not just the unofficial kickoff to summer in the United States. It's an important day when we remember those who have given their lives in service to their country. If you have members of your own family who have served in the military and passed away, either in the line of duty or as veterans, you have a perfect introduction for discussing this topic with your children. Even if you do not have this personal connection to the military, you can help your children appreciate the sacrifices of those who have served in the armed forces. During an otherwise fun-filled Memorial Day weekend, consider taking your children to a local veterans' cemetery and talking about the people who are being remembered there. If you and your family would like to help place flags, Michael Freeman offers the following advice in his article for the Bryan on Scouting blog, "Guidance for Honoring Veterans with Grave Site Flags on Memorial Day":

- Contact the cemetery director ahead of time so she can direct your efforts.
- Learn the correct way to place flags. For example, in the United States, place each flag about a foot in front of the center of the headstone.
- Use correct flag etiquette (for example, never let a flag touch the ground).
- Of course, show respect.

If you are interested in laying a wreath (you can also do this during the end-of-year holidays), Wreaths Across America (https://www.wreathsacrossamerica.org) can provide information and support.

June

National Hunger Awareness Month and National Hunger Awareness Day (June 6)

Hunger and food insecurity are important topics to introduce to children as they begin to appreciate how fortunate they are to have enough food, as many people do not. By interacting with food pantries, soup kitchens, and food-recovery organizations, children learn how important it is to be mindful of food waste and to help others who might not have enough to eat. Try working with No Kid Hungry (https://www.nokidhungry.org), which works to end childhood hunger in the United States through breakfast, after-school, and summer meal programs; food skills education; and advocacy.

June 1: International Children's Day and the International Day for Protection of Children

According to Compassion International, these events are dedicated to celebrating children and raising awareness of the welfare issues they face. You can take this opportunity to talk as a family about problems that affect many children around the world, such as lack of education, clean water, and health care. Here are a few organizations to work with that focus on children:

- Save the Children (https://www.savethechildren.org)
- Pencils of Promise (https://pencilsofpromise.org)
- UNICEF (https://www.unicef.org)

Father's Day (date varies)

Like Mother's Day, Father's Day is celebrated in many countries on varying dates. In the United States, it is celebrated on the third Sunday in June. Take this special day to show love and appreciation for the fathers, grandfathers, uncles, cousins, caregivers, and other important men in your children's lives. Father figures and caregivers don't need fancy gifts or expensive outings to feel loved and appreciated. A homemade card expressing genuine sentiments of admiration and gratitude or a special song or poem (perhaps performed or recited while serving breakfast in bed) would be appreciated by anyone being celebrated on Father's Day. Thoughtful arts-and-crafts projects, such as handprint cards, handmade superhero capes, or a "World's Best Dad" certificate, are easily made. (Many other creative ideas can be found online.)

Engaging in service together is another wonderful way to honor Dad and make him proud of the kindhearted, generous family he is raising. Any of your favorite volunteer efforts, such as serving in a soup kitchen, helping an elderly or ill neighbor, or working in a local community garden, are wonderful ways to spend quality time together. Instead of giving gifts, consider donating to a cause close to the recipient's heart, or try purchasing a gift that gives back, through a website such as Uncommon Goods (https://www.uncommongoods.com).

June 20: World Refugee Day

In recent years, the number of refugees and displaced people around the world has surpassed sixty million, a number that the United Nations High Commission for Refugees says symbolizes "'immense human suffering.'" While this is a difficult issue for young children to understand, there are gentle ways to talk about helping people who are displaced from their homes. There are many excellent organizations to work with to help refugees meet their basic needs:

- UNICEF (https://www.unicef.org)
- The International Rescue Committee (https://www.rescue.org)
- Oxfam International (https://www.oxfam.org)
- Save the Children (https://www.savethechildren.org)
- Mercy Corps (https://www.mercycorps.org)

If refugees have settled in your community, check with local government authorities, churches, and schools to find out how you and your family can assist. These newcomers often need help acquiring basic household supplies, learning the local language, or simply navigating their new neighborhoods.

July

July 4: Independence Day

Similar events: Constitution Memorial Day (Japan, May 3), Canada Day (July 1), Bastille Day (France, July 14), and individual independence celebrations in many countries (various dates)

In the United States, this favorite summer holiday is filled with food, parties, and fireworks. Many communities also host parades that honor veterans, military members, and first responders. Attending and cheering for these folks is a great way to remind children to be respectful and grateful to the men and women who have served and who continue to keep us safe. Service projects that support soldiers or that benefit your community (see "Community-Service Ideas for Playdates" on page 15) are also appropriate around this holiday.

July 24: Camp Kindness Day

Many children around the world spend parts of their summers at day or sleepaway camps. In the United States, the American Camp Association, in collaboration with Kindness Evolution (https://www.kindnessevolution.org), has created Camp Kindness Day (https://www.acacamps.org/camp-kindness-day), a day when summer camps across the country focus their activities and programs on intentional acts of kindness and care. If your children are campers, encourage them to do a few small acts of kindness for fellow campers and staff on this day and, even better, throughout their camp experiences. You can send your children a few stacks of colorful sticky notes and encourage them to write loving notes to bunkmates, fellow campers, and counselors and leave them in cubbies or on pillows. Send your campers some colorful thread along with alphabet beads and instructions for creating friendship bracelets (a summer-camp staple). Be sure to emphasize reaching out to new friends or to those who seem to be having a hard time with homesickness.

July 30: International Day of Friendship

This United Nations observance honors the role that friendship plays in promoting peace. Be on the lookout for events in your community, or consider hosting a friendship party for your children and their friends. Children can make simple friendship bracelets for each other, write complimentary notes to one another (for example, "You are a great friend because _____."), or create flowers out of construction paper and write one characteristic of a good friend on each petal.

August

National Eye Exam Month

This event can be especially meaningful if someone in your family wears glasses or contact lenses. Help your children understand how fortunate they are to have access to proper eye care, which is too expensive or unavailable for many people around the world. The Lions Club Recycle for Sight program (http://www.lionsclubs.org/EN/how-we-serve/health/sight/eyeglass-recycling.php) collects used eyeglasses and distributes them to people in need. Consider gathering old eyeglasses from family members and friends to donate.

First Tuesday in August: National Night Out

In the United States, National Night Out (https://natw.org/) is held annually to unify neighborhoods and build partnerships between police and the people they serve. Communities nationwide host block parties, safety demonstrations, youth events, visits from emergency personnel, and cookouts to bring law enforcement and neighbors together in a positive environment. While not specifically focused on volunteering, National Night Out is a great way to promote kindness, develop relationships, and foster a sense of community. If your town doesn't have an event, you can learn how to create and register one on the website, or you can work with your neighbors to throw your own block party to build neighborhood unity.

August 17: National Nonprofit Day

In the United States, National Nonprofit Day shines a spotlight on the many charitable organizations around the country that pursue specific altruistic goals, such as raising awareness of social-justice issues, supporting research, and providing aid to those in need, as well as highlighting these organizations' positive effects on communities. You can take this opportunity to work with your children to explore the many nonprofits in your community and determine the ones that you'd like to support with your time and resources during the upcoming school year.

August 21: Senior Citizens Day

Similar events: Respect of the Aged Day (Japan, third Monday in September), International Day of Older Persons (October 1)

Senior Citizens Day serves as a reminder to reach out to elderly family members, neighbors, or friends. Schedule a visit to your local senior center or nursing home to deliver cards or paper flowers. Arrange a bingo game, host a sing-along, or, if it is allowed, bring along a gentle pet.

September

Childhood Cancer Awareness Month

There are many ways for children to support other children who are battling serious illnesses. Here are a few organizations that offer ideas for how you and your children can help:

- Alex's Lemonade Stand Foundation (https://www.alexslemonade.org)
- Send Kids the World (www.sendkidstheworld.com)
- Make-A-Wish (http://wish.org)
- Project Linus (www.projectlinus.org)
- Tiny Superheroes (https://tinysuperheroes.com)
- Cards for Hospitalized Kids (www.cardsforhospitalizedkids.com)

First Monday in September: Labor Day

Similar events: Celebrated as Workers' Day in many countries on varying dates (typically May 1)

According to the US Department of Labor, Labor Day celebrates American workers' accomplishments. In the United States and Canada, most people have the day off. Of course, many people such as healthcare workers, farmers, first responders, and parents are required to work on this holiday. Spending some time volunteering with your children on Labor Day is a nice way to acknowledge and thank all of those who work to make the country strong. Your family can deliver cookies and notes of gratitude to your local firehouse or police station, or if you live near a farm, you can reach out and ask whether volunteers can help on Labor Day.

Since it falls on the last official weekend of summer, Labor Day also offers a great opportunity to hold a lemonade stand or car wash for charity. As mentioned earlier, September is a perfect time to support childhood cancer research, and Alex's Lemonade Stand Foundation (https://www.alexslemonade.org) provides excellent resources to make your lemonade stand a success.

First Sunday after Labor Day: Grandparents Day

We certainly don't need a holiday to celebrate, honor, and connect with grandparents and other special seniors in our children's lives, but Grandparents Day is an opportunity to schedule a special visit to a senior center or nursing home to deliver cards, cookies, or paper flowers. As families scatter across the country and fewer grandparents live near grandchildren, most institutionalized elderly people receive very few visits from family and friends. You and your children can make a big impact on the lives of these seniors with a friendly visit or card delivery.

September 11: National Day of Service and Remembrance

In the United States, according to the Corporation for National and Community Service, this day is an opportunity to give back in honor of those who were affected by the terrorist attacks of September 11, 2001. While this day brings up difficult issues to discuss with young children, it is nevertheless a chance to engage in acts of kindness, particularly for first responders in your community.

Several organizations provide information and volunteer opportunities related to this observance:

- 9/11 Day (https://www.911day.org)
- Corporation for National and Community Service (https://www.nationalservice.gov/serve/september-11th-national-day-service-and-remembrance)
- Points of Light (www.pointsoflight.org)
- 9/11 Memorial and Museum (https://www.911memorial.org/museum)

October

October 1: National Homemade Cookies Day

Celebrate this sweet holiday by making cookies for friends, neighbors, and people who are lonely. Even better, try a new recipe for a friend with special dietary needs that prevent her from eating traditional homemade cookies.

October 5: World Day of Bullying Prevention

Children are never too young to begin talking about kindness, compassion, and inclusiveness, and it's important to give them the tools to speak out if they witness bullying. There are many great children's books that speak to children about the importance of standing up for others. On this day, children can be encouraged to leave kind, supportive notes for classmates on their desks or in their cubbies. For more ideas on what children can do, see StopBullying.gov (https://www.stopbullying.gov/kids/what-you-can-do/index.html).

October 31: Halloween

Halloween is a child-focused holiday that provides many opportunities for spreading sweetness. Consider sharing the fun by gathering used costumes, donating leftover candy to the Candy Give-Back program through Operation Gratitude (https://www.operationgratitude.com) or collecting donations through Trick-or-Treat for UNICEF (https://www.unicefusa.org/trick-or-treat). See chapter 7 for details about each of these projects.

November

First Tuesday after November 1: Election Day

In the United States, many schools are used as polling stations, so Election Day is often a day off from school. This special day is a great time to talk about democracy, civics, and social justice. While it may be hard for children to understand their ability to effect change in our government, there are advocacy projects you can do as a family that will spark conversations about participatory government. You can write letters to your local or state representatives about issues of concern in your community or engage in e-advocacy (emailing or participating in online polls and petitions). The Doing Good Together website offers other ideas for advocating for peace, justice, and social action on its "Pick a Project" page (https://www.doinggoodtogether.org/bhf/pick-a-project).

November 11: Veterans Day

Similar events: also called Armistice Day or Remembrance Day (various countries), Remembrance Sunday (United Kingdom, closest Sunday to November 11)

According to the US Department of Veterans Affairs, Veterans Day honors all who have served in the American military. If there is a parade in your town, bring your children to clap and wave at the veterans who march. Support the military and veterans through sending care packages, letters and cards, stuffed animals, candy, and books, all of which are all deeply appreciated by the men and women who are serving far away from home and family. More suggestions for supporting veterans and the military are discussed in "Service Ideas for Summer" in chapter 7.

Saturday Before Thanksgiving: Family Volunteer Day

The Points of Light Foundation, GenerationON, and Disney all support this day of families serving together. Check the Points of Light Foundation (www.pointsoflight.org) and GenerationON (https://www.generationon.org) websites for Family Volunteer Day projects and events in your area.

Fourth Thursday in November: Thanksgiving

Similar events: Saint Lucia, first Monday in October; Canada, second Monday in October; Liberia, first Thursday in November; Labor Thanksgiving Day (Japan, November 23); Harvest Thanksgiving Festival (India, Sri Lanka, Malaysia, mid-January)

This holiday is the perfect time to focus your family on gratitude, compassion, and service. So many Americans are hungry or food insecure, including up to 13 million children, according to No Kid Hungry, and food drives are common at Thanksgiving. The entire month of November can be dedicated to expressing gratitude for our many blessings and helping the hungry. See chapter 7 for details about several Thanksgiving-themed service projects.

Tuesday after Thanksgiving: Giving Tuesday

Giving Tuesday (https://www.givingtuesday.org) is a unique giving holiday (as opposed to the shopping holidays of Black Friday and Cyber Monday) and represents a global giving movement, fueled by social media and community collaboration. Americans are encouraged to give time and resources to charities they care about on Giving Tuesday, which unofficially kicks off the charitable giving season. The Giving Tuesday website offers a searchable directory of organizations in your community that would welcome your family's support.

December

December 5: International Ninja Day

This tongue-in-cheek holiday is a great opportunity to quickly and stealthily make someone smile. Help children slip a kind note into someone's mailbox, ding-dong-ditch a treat on a neighbor's doorstep, or secretly perform a chore such as shoveling snow or straightening a room for someone else.

December "Giving" Holidays: Hanukkah (dates vary) and Christmas (December 25)

These holidays offer your family the chance to consider the needs of others while you shop, cook, bake, wrap, and celebrate this joyful time of year. Chapter 7 describes many different ways to incorporate service meaningfully into this season. By doing so, you'll ensure that children are grateful for what they are given, and you'll be creating family memories that will last long after the last cookie is eaten, the wrapping paper is cleaned up, and the decorations are stored away. In addition to local toy drives organized by your community or house of worship, there are many national organizations established to help you share the joy of these holidays with children and families in need. Here are some organizations to consider working with:

- The Marine Corps Toys for Tots Program (https://www.toysfortots.org)
- Macy's Believe Campaign benefiting Make-A-Wish (https://www.macys.com/social/believe)

- Operation Santa through the US Postal Service (https://about.usps.com/holidaynews/operation-santa.htm)
- Operation Christmas Child through Samaritan's Purse (https://www.samaritanspurse.org/what-we-do/operation-christmas-child/)
- Ronald McDonald House (https://www.rmhc.org)
- Operation Holiday Joy through the Armed Services YMCA (https://www.asymca.org/operation-holiday-joy/)
- St. Jude Children's Research Hospital (https://www.stjude.org)
- Operation Warm (https://www.operationwarm.org)

December 31: New Year's Eve

In addition to celebrating with food, drink, hats, and noisemakers, consider working with your children to show gratitude to the many people who have made a positive impact in your family's life over the previous year. Create thank-you cards or small gifts for the postal carrier, the daycare provider, the doorman, or the bus driver on your route. You can also spend a few minutes, as you did on Thanksgiving, talking to your children about all of the people and things for which they are grateful and adding notes about these to your gratitude jar (see chapter 7 for more information on gratitude jars). Finally, many cultures and religions ring in the new year by attending religious services, giving thanks in their own ways for the many blessings of the previous year. In the morning, you can work on your service-related resolutions for the new year!

Share, Reflect, and Keep It Going

When my children were young, I heard a very true—and sometimes overused—adage: "The days are long, but the years are short" (recently popularized by author Gretchen Rubin). As author Anna Quindlen said, we get so caught up in getting things done for our young children on a daily basis that we miss the big picture, the beauty, and the memories to be made in the *doing*. As I prepare to send my oldest child off to college soon, I am keenly aware of this truth and wish I had many of those long days to relive.

The life of a child is guided by many different calendars and timetables, including school calendars, holidays, annual pediatric checkups, school breaks, and summer vacations, which dictate the ebb and flow of our days as families. Taking a moment at the end of each month to look ahead and get an overview of the coming month is a great practice. It gives you a chance to anticipate the pockets of time where you might insert activities to promote connection, reflection, and family service. Modern technology affords us many tools to help manage our time and remember important dates, ensuring that every holiday, birthday, anniversary, and other milestone is noted, with alarms set to remind us to take notice.

The goal of this book is to make family service easy and accessible and to help you begin to think outside of the box for ways that your family can volunteer and spread goodness together. You absolutely need not feel pressured to make time to engage in service if you are overwhelmed and can't approach an activity with an open heart and a positive attitude. My hope is that this chapter provides new information and inspiration, giving you the spark of an idea for incorporating kindness and service into things you are already doing. You can do it by living your family's values with purpose, keeping it simple, using a little creativity and imagination, and considering every age and developmental stage in your family.

SIMPLE ACTS IN ACTION: SPREADING KINDNESS ON SEPTEMBER 11

My family and I live in New York City, and one of our most cherished family traditions has turned the anniversary of a tragedy into a day of fond remembrance, kindness, and hope.

No one who is old enough to remember the terrorist attacks of September 11, 2001, will ever forget that day—particularly the residents of New York City. As the first anniversary of the attacks approached, I wanted to acknowledge the day in a way that felt hopeful and showed gratitude to the first responders who had given and suffered so much. So I baked some cookies, made some cards of thanks, put eighteen-month-old Emi in her stroller, and set out for our local firehouse and police station. The gifts were received with thanks, and at the firehouse, I lifted Emi out to visit with the firefighters and their Dalmatian, Yogi. This outing lightened hearts all around on what was otherwise a day of sad remembrance.

As the years have passed, my family has turned these deliveries into a tradition. Though the morning of September 11 brings all off-duty city firefighters to a memorial service at the 9/11 Memorial and Museum, the doors of firehouses typically remain open for visitors in the afternoon. If the anniversary falls on a school day, my children and I make our visits after school lets out and bring friends along. Recently, we visited our local police precinct and found notes we had written more than a decade earlier still displayed on the bulletin board. This small gesture is always warmly received, especially as time passes and many people don't even pause to acknowledge the day. It's a great way to remind my children to be grateful for the helpers in our community whom we often take for granted and that expressing that gratitude, even in the smallest way, is appreciated.

CHAPTER **FIVE**
Kindness Day by Day

> "In a world where you can be anything, be kind."
> —Unknown

The transformative power of service, and the belief that one person *can* make a difference, are concepts increasingly promoted on social media. It is heartening to see that people and organizations are beginning to focus on spreading positive, hopeful messages. For parents, every new day offers an opportunity to model this attitude for our children through considerate and thoughtful interactions with other people and the world around us. Over time, these daily acts can become lifelong habits of kindness.

To help your children build their own habits of service, find some way to record, track, and celebrate your daily kind actions. The Doing Good Together website offers "kindness challenge" sheets which can be printed and hung on the refrigerator. You might also consider leaving a colorful journal in your kitchen or front hall so that your children can jot down the good deeds they have done each week. Or you could hang a wall calendar, place a small sticker on the appropriate day each time someone does something helpful or kind, and count up the stickers each month.

So what exactly will you be tracking? The possibilities are endless. Chapters 1 through 4 offer ideas for special occasions, but many smaller, spontaneous opportunities for service arise each day. To take advantage of these little moments, here is my own list of many simple acts of kindness that can be done with young children and easily fit into a busy family schedule.

These ideas are categorized by where or whom you serve, but they need not be carried out in a particular order. Choose one or two to start with, and let them inspire you to try others or to come up with your own simple acts of everyday service.

Kindness Begins at Home

There are lots of kindness activities you can do with your children right from your own kitchen table. For example, make a colorful thank-you note for the mail carrier or the trash collectors, and leave it in your mailbox or taped to the top of your garbage can. Consider occasionally hiding a little note of love and support in your children's lunch boxes or backpacks. Encourage them to do the same for siblings or friends at school. Create a birdfeeder together, place it outside a window, and ask your children to be in charge of making sure it is refilled as needed. During dinner or at bedtime, ask each child to name one thing for which he is thankful or one nice thing he did for another person that day.

While kindness begins at home, its effects can ripple beyond your walls. Offer to pick up groceries or items at the pharmacy for a neighbor who is facing a health crisis or has welcomed a new family member, and take your children with you. On a snowy day, encourage your children to bring hot chocolate to a family member, neighbor, or paid helper who is shoveling snow around your home. Pick a quiet day and time (perhaps Sunday evening before dinner) to regularly call or video-chat with a faraway relative. Even if you leave a message, you will brighten that person's day. When your children receive gifts for birthdays or holidays, encourage them to send handwritten thank-you notes to the givers right away. If your children are too young to write their own messages, compose a few sentences for them, and ask them to sign their names and decorate the notes.

Out in the Community

Even during the busyness of errands and other out-and-about activities, you can slip in some service. For instance, smile at, make eye contact with, and greet as many people as you can as you walk through your day with your children. If someone holds the door, say thank you and remind your children to do the same. If your children are old enough, encourage them to hold doors for others. Learn the names of people you and your children encounter frequently—baristas at the coffee shop, security guards at the bank, desk clerks at the dry cleaner, cashiers at the grocery store, and so on—and use their names when you greet them. It makes a difference.

At school, there are all sorts of chances to thank people whose efforts often go unacknowledged. Help your children deliver a hot drink to a crossing guard on a cold or rainy day (or a cold drink on a hot day) as you make your way to or from school. Send your children to school with colorful sticky-note pads, and encourage them to leave kind notes on the desks or in the cubbies of classmates and teachers. Remind them to also leave notes for security guards, school nurses, office secretaries, and cafeteria workers— all of the people who make the school safe and special.

You can brighten someone's day for the price of a cup of coffee (or even less). For instance, let your children see you pay for the person behind you in the drive-through line or toll booth. If you and your children are in a coffee-shop line in front of a police officer, firefighter, or EMT, quietly give the cashier some extra money and tell him you are anonymously paying for the civil servant behind you. At a deli, an ice-cream parlor, or another establishment with a tip jar, let your children put in a few coins. They will likely get a smile and a hearty thank-you from the person behind the counter.

Opportunities for kindness are all over your community, including outdoors. Pick up litter on family strolls through neighborhoods, parks, or green spaces. Talk with your children about how it is everyone's responsibility to keep the earth clean. If you and your children walk your dog together, carry extra treats. As you encounter other dogs on the street or in the park, encourage your children to ask the owners whether it would be okay to pet the other dogs or give them treats.

Helping Those Less Fortunate

Serving those who are experiencing hard times fosters compassion, empathy, and gratitude in children. Together, sort through gently used children's books, and create a pile to donate. Do the same with mittens, hats, scarves, and coats in the winter months or gently used clothing during other changes of season. Write or draw small notes of love and encouragement to put in the pockets or between the pages of donated items for the recipients to find.

Other items around your home can also be turned into service projects. Have your children help you sort through your stash of unopened travel-sized and hotel toiletries, and create care kits for a local homeless shelter or food pantry. Keep a few of these kits, along with some granola bars, in your car, or carry them in your bag or stroller, to have on hand if you encounter a homeless person during your daily travels with your children. Create a giving jar or box, and encourage your children to fill it with loose change they find around your home. At the end of the year or when the jar is full, hold a family meeting to decide which charity will receive the money you've collected.

Your local food pantry provides an ongoing service opportunity that you can approach in creative ways. While grocery shopping, instruct your children to keep their eyes open for nonperishable items on sale; for example, boxes of pasta or cans of vegetables are often sold as buy one, get one half price. Pick up extra items as you are able, and deliver them to your local food pantry. Every three months or so, sort through your own pantry and collect unopened items to donate. If you can't spare any food, count the number of items in your pantry, and donate a small amount of money, such as a quarter or a dime, for each one. Your children can do the counting and work on the math to come up with the total donation amount. If the food pantry will accept decorated nonperishables, buy some round sticky labels and ask your children to draw colorful smiley faces on them. Attach them to the tops of the cans and jars you are donating. They are sure to make the recipients smile.

Even a little screen time can spread kindness. Help your children log on to Free Rice (http://freerice.com), where they can play games and earn points to donate rice to hungry children around the world.

Anytime, Anywhere

Some acts of kindness can be completed no matter where you are or what else you are doing. Give an honest compliment to a friend or stranger, and let your children hear you. If you shop on Amazon, enroll in Amazon Smile (https://smile.amazon.com/), and explain to your children how this program donates a portion of the cost of your purchases to a charity of your choice.

Loved ones appreciate small gestures that show you are thinking of them. Have children mark a wall calendar in bright colors to help you remember birthdays and anniversaries. On these special days, reach out together to the applicable friends and family members through cards, texts, emails, or phone calls. If you take photos of your children doing something great—performing in a show, playing in a soccer game, receiving awards—ask if they'd like to share the photos of their special day with a faraway relative. Let your children decide which photos to make into prints, and encourage them to write the note that will accompany the photos.

Even sad events provide opportunities to serve. If a neighbor or friend suffers the death of a loved one or pet, talk to your children about ways that you could help the person feel better. Grief and loss are difficult for young children to process, but if you bring your children along to purchase flowers or encourage them to write simple notes to the grieving person, you are helping them develop the empathy they will need throughout their lives to appropriately interact with people who are hurting.

Share, Reflect, and Keep It Going

It may seem like the acts of kindness listed in this chapter are obvious examples of everyday interactions with others. That may be true for your family, but the reality is that many people are understandably consumed by their own schedules and troubles and spend so much time focusing on themselves or on the screens in front of them that they forget to look around and appreciate the needs of others. Greeting the people we encounter with a positive attitude, a smile, and a helping hand brings joy to others, and these very basic activities also make us feel better, happier, and more connected.

As you rush through your busy days with children, it might be hard to keep in mind the guiding principles of meaningful service, but these small acts of kindness form the basis of your family's kindness practice. Simplicity is the key. It's not a big deal to remind our children to hold the door for the next person or to leave a few coins in the tip jar at the coffee shop. As soon as you've done these things a few times, children will begin to do them on their own without prompting.

Occasionally, you might want to go beyond your day-to-day routines and encourage your children to perform more involved acts of kindness, such as making a card for your postal worker or delivering flowers to a grieving friend. While these special activities take additional time and might not be possible every day, they will likely elicit deep appreciation from the recipients, who will recognize the efforts you've made. These events provide additional opportunities to talk with your children about ways they might like to help another person or show gratitude. Kind actions build and strengthen relationships with the people who populate your child's world by showing neighbors, helpers, and public servants that you see them, acknowledge their assistance, and value their feelings.

Whatever service you add to your regular routines, you are organically finding purpose in your day-to-day life. Obviously, each simple act that you do throughout the day does not require reflection or discussion; you do not need to ask children to express their feelings about every positive interaction they have. Children will simply begin to understand that kindness, generosity, and helpfulness are the ways in which your family navigates the world.

As mentioned in the introduction to this chapter, it is fun to take some time at the end of each day, such as over dinner or at bath time, to ask each child to name one kind thing he did for another person that day or one way in which he was a helper. You can also ask each child to name the one thing for which he is most grateful today. Thinking about and expressing gratitude naturally makes us feel happier and more grateful.

SIMPLE ACTS IN ACTION: ALAINA AND BEAR

Almost since she uttered her first words, my daughter Alaina has been obsessed with dogs. I believe that some people are born animal lovers, and that is certainly the case with Alaina.

We rescued a terrier, Patty, a few years ago to satisfy Alaina's longing for a pet, and she adores the animal. She also loves (and can name) all of the other dogs in our large apartment building.

Shortly after moving in, we befriended a woman named Milena, who had a sweet old dog named Bear. Alaina delighted in petting Bear, who was very slow and gentle, and Milena became a friend with whom we would chat in the hallway, lobby, and elevator. Sadly, Bear's health gradually deteriorated, and we were concerned to learn he had a brain tumor and was losing his sight. Milena took great care of him, even finding a specialist who performed surgery to remove the tumor with limited success. But Bear passed away after a few months.

I heard the news from one of the building staff members and had to break it to Alaina, who was only nine years old at the time. She was confused and upset, as it was her first real experience with death. We talked about what we could do to help Milena during this sad time. I suggested that Alaina could make her a card, and we bought a bouquet of flowers. The card included a beautiful, detailed drawing that Alaina had made of Bear, and Alaina expressed her sadness over his loss, telling Milena what a special dog he had been. We left the note and flowers at Milena's door, as we didn't want to disturb her.

A few days later, I ran into Milena in our lobby. She expressed her thanks with tears in her eyes. She had been very moved by our kind gesture, but she had been overwhelmed at Alaina's message of sympathy and the beautiful drawing she had made of Bear. We still visit Milena (she has since rescued a new dog), and Alaina's drawing of Bear is proudly displayed in Milena's kitchen.

Speaking to children about death is never easy, but we need to teach them the important life skills of reaching out to those who are hurting and appropriately expressing sympathy. Our gesture toward Milena took us just a few minutes, but it made us feel better to express our sadness about Bear's loss, and it clearly meant a great deal to our neighbor.

CHAPTER **SIX**
Taking Service on the Road

"Just to travel is rather boring. But to travel with a purpose is educational and exciting."
—Sargent Shriver, American diplomat, politician, and activist

Whether you are driving a few hours from home or flying to a faraway location, you can find ways to incorporate kindness and service into your family's vacation adventures. Traveling with children introduces them to the diversity and beauty in the world and exposes them to new cultures, traditions, and languages. It also provides an opportunity to spread a little joy to the people you encounter along the way and, if you volunteer at your destination, to contribute meaningfully to the community you are visiting.

A "destination" service trip is great but certainly not necessary. You don't need to spend money or venture far to make a difference. Small, intentional acts of kindness can be incorporated into any family trip. They help to pass the time and lighten the mood during restless hours of travel.

If you want service to be a bigger part of your vacation, consider working with a voluntourism organization to make your plans. There are more than 300 voluntourism companies worldwide that promote opportunities to combine travel and service. Some organizations offer all-inclusive experience packages, while others connect you with local organizations for free or a small fee. The majority of these experiences attract single travelers, but a 2015 report authored by Lynn Minnaert found that 10 percent of families have taken a voluntourism trip and 29 percent of families say they're likely to take such a trip in the future. This chapter lists ideas, destinations, and voluntourism companies to inspire you as you incorporate service into your next family vacation.

Kindness Activities for Any Trip

When you have a long car ride or flight ahead of you, find some space in your bags of snacks, books, and devices for a few easy kindness projects.

Pretrip Preparation

Before you depart, gather some simple supplies for on-the-go service:

- Construction or colored paper
- Colorful sticky notes
- Colored pencils or crayons
- Postcard stamps (available at the post office)
- Printed templates for cards, letters, postcards, and windshield poetry
- Address labels for relatives and charities

Research your destination and any communities you will visit along the way to find family-friendly volunteer opportunities there. Let your children have input on this part of your vacation. Ask them which of the options they'd most like to do and how they'd like to help others while on your trip. Any time children contribute to the planning for service, they are more engaged and invested.

Kindness En Route

- Leave poetry on windshields. Car Window Poetry (https://www.carwindowpoetry.com) is an online community that invites you to share encouraging poems with strangers. The founder, Alex Lewis, says you can "make a big difference in people's lives through small acts of love." I couldn't agree more. To join the Car Window Poetry effort, follow these instructions:
  - Download Car Window Poetry cards from the website, and cut them apart.
  - Work with your children to write short poems in the car during long rides, while waiting for food in restaurants, or whenever you have some downtime.
  - Place the poems on the windows of cars you encounter in rest stops, gas stations, and parking lots throughout your vacation.
- If writing poetry is not your family's strength, leave simple, cheerful notes on windshields instead.
- Send postcards. The practice of sending a vacation postcard has almost completely faded away with the rise of text, email, and social-media posting. My extended family is a little more old-school, and they still enjoy sending and receiving postcards—and your loved ones probably will too. Bring along some postcard stamps and preprinted address labels (easier than fitting handwritten addresses on small postcards), and buy postcards when you reach your destination. Ask your children to write a few words or draw pictures on each postcard, and then send the cards to faraway loved ones. They'll be thrilled, even if they receive the postcards after you have long since returned home.

- Write encouraging notes. Suggest that children write notes and cards of encouragement to soldiers, veterans, children battling illness, or anyone who could use a smile. For some ideas of organizations that will accept these cards, see "Make Cards and Letters of Encouragement and Gratitude" on page 11 and "Military Appreciation Month" on page 52. You could also donate cards to charities in your home community or at your vacation destination.
- Thank someone who helps you. Every interaction with a hotel maid, a waitress, a gas-station attendant, or an amusement-park worker is an opportunity to smile, make eye contact, wish the person a nice day, and express sincere gratitude for their help and service. Consider leaving a complimentary handwritten note on a restaurant check if the server was particularly kind, or write a note on hotel stationery for the cleaning staff who service your room after you check out.
- Pick up litter. It may seem obvious, but encourage children to pick up after themselves wherever you go, and try to pick up any litter that you see in parks or on beaches. National parks and campgrounds frequently encourage guests to leave no trace. This should be the mantra no matter where we take our children.

 Quick Kindness Tip: Screen Time on Vacations

While devices help pass the time during long hours of travel, excessive screen time can limit the effect of service experiences and hinder memory making during vacations. For example, my husband and I took our children on a car trip when they were small. As we drove up a mountain and spotted an incredible view of the Pacific Ocean, Jonathan and I tried to get the children's attention by shouting, "Look at *that*!" Our son, Archie, was so engrossed in his electronic device that when he did look up, he looked out the wrong window—into the side of the mountain—and said in an unimpressed tone, "Wow."

Vacation is a great time to disconnect from our devices and reconnect with each other. All family members will get more out of the trip and naturally find more ways to spread kindness and give back to the local community if they are looking up, observing, and appreciating all that is around them.

Kindness Activities for Travel in the United States

Try adding these hotel chains, destinations, and voluntourism companies to your service plans when you and your family are traveling within the United States.

American Hotel Chains with Service Programs

Many popular hotel chains have established programs that encourage civic responsibility. I've listed some in this section, but even if you are staying at a different chain, ask your concierge whether that hotel sponsors a similar program or whether she is aware of one in the area.

Omni Hotels and Resorts (https://www.omnihotels.com) sponsors a campaign called Say Goodnight to Hunger. For every reservation made at a participating Omni Hotel, one meal is donated to a family in need in the local community. Omni associates also donate thousands of volunteer hours to local food banks and hunger charities. Many Omni Hotel properties have developed relationships with local food banks where guests can volunteer. Some age restrictions may apply, depending on the facility.

Ritz-Carlton Resorts (www.myritzcarltonclub.com/en-us/getaways.jsp) has developed Ritz-Carlton Give Back Getaways at its properties in St. Thomas, US Virgin Islands; the state of Colorado; and San Francisco, California. The program offers members of the Ritz-Carlton Destination Club an opportunity to give back through half-day local community experiences. Working alongside Ritz-Carlton staff, guests can engage in projects related to child welfare, hunger relief, or conservation.

Destinations in the United States with Service Programs

Best Friends Animal Sanctuary (https://bestfriends.org) in Kanab, Utah, is the largest no-kill pet sanctuary in the United States. If you have animal lovers in your family and your travels take you to Utah, you can coordinate a visit to volunteer at Best Friends. If you can't make it to Kanab but would like to work with animals in another area, the Best Friends website provides links to regional programs in Salt Lake City, Utah; Los Angeles, California; New York City, New York; and Atlanta, Georgia. The website also hosts a searchable database of other animal-rescue organizations and shelters across the United States that might welcome young volunteers.

America's national parks are perfect destinations for a family that cares about the environment and enjoys the outdoors:

- Through the National Parks Volunteer Program (https://www.nps.gov/getinvolved/volunteer.htm), volunteers of all ages are welcome at most national parks, and you can search for appropriate opportunities on the website. All children under age eighteen must be accompanied by an adult and in many cases must have a signed waiver.

- The Junior Ranger program (https://www.nps.gov/kids/jrRangers.cfm) is available in almost all national parks. To become Junior Rangers, children participate in activities at a park and talk with a ranger about what they have discovered. Junior Rangers learn about the parks, how to protect them, and how to keep them clean and safe for visitors.

- The Sierra Club, the largest grassroots environmental organization in the United States, offers "adventures with a cause"—trips for families that include rafting, hiking, and backpacking as well as service. These tours typically run during the summer months in California, Utah, Idaho, Colorado, Oregon, and other states. For more information, see https://content.sierraclub.org/outings/adventure-travel.

- Give Kids the World Village (http://www.gktw.org/) is an 84-acre nonprofit resort in Kissimmee, Florida, run by volunteers called *angels*, to provide a free, week-long vacation and access to Walt Disney World for children with life-threatening illnesses and their families. Vacationing families in Central Florida can take three- or four-hour volunteer shifts any day of the week. Families must complete an application to become angels, and the minimum age for participation in most activities is twelve, but some opportunities welcome younger children. The long list of volunteer activities includes scooping ice cream, staffing rides such as the carousel, participating in evening entertainment, and wearing costumes to bring beloved characters to life.

- Animal lovers and future farmers might enjoy volunteering at a Farm Sanctuary (https://www.farmsanctuary.org/) location. One property is in upstate New York, and one is in Northern California. With a mission of protecting farm animals from cruelty and promoting compassionate vegan living, Farm Sanctuary offers a unique way for your family to help animals. Some age requirements apply for most volunteer opportunities, but the website offers detailed information and additional resources for families interested in vegetarianism and farm-animal rescue.

- Youth Rebuilding New Orleans (http://yrno.com) is a grassroots organization that engages youth groups and families in helping to rebuild distressed and foreclosed homes in New Orleans. The refurbished homes are sold to teachers to stabilize neighborhoods. This activity is geared toward older children and teens, but families with younger children are welcome to participate, and YRNO has become a popular service-vacation destination for families visiting New Orleans. All minors must have a signed waiver and must be accompanied by a parent at all times.

Voluntourism Companies in the United States

- The Nature Corps (www.thenaturecorps.org) offers award-winning, all-inclusive volunteer vacations. On trips to Yosemite and Sequoia National Parks, among other destinations, volunteers work to preserve national and state parks.

- Together for Good (https://wp.togetherforgood.org/OLD/) provides specific ideas for family-oriented service travel (to both domestic and international locations) and occasionally coordinates group trips.
- Visit.org (https://visit.org/worldwide) is an online marketplace that offers a variety of purposeful, hands-on travel tours and workshops through hundreds of nonprofit organizations in several dozen countries, including the United States. The focus is on short (half-day to one-day), affordable experiences that give back to local communities.

 Quick Kindness Tip: Pack Some Extra Love

If you can spare a little space in your luggage, you can help people in need in the city you are visiting. Pack for a Purpose (https://www.packforapurpose.org) provides specific supply lists of needed items to travelers who want to make a meaningful contribution to destinations they visit in all parts of the world. The lists are created by working with local community-based organizations, so you can be sure that the items you are packing will be put to good use. The website allows you to search for a destination and connect with a local tour company, hotel, or resort. It also provides wish-list items for specific programs in that location, along with instructions on how to drop off the items once you arrive. An informational video on the website shows how to efficiently fit items into your bag.

Kindness Activities for International Travel

Try adding these hotel chains and voluntourism companies to your service plans when you and your family are traveling internationally.

International Hotel Chains with Service Programs

- Sandals Resorts (https://sandalsfoundation.org) sponsors the Reading Road Trip to boost children's literacy in the Caribbean. Operated through Island Routes Adventure Tours (https://www.islandroutes.com/island-impact), this program allows guests at Sandals, Beaches (https://www.beaches.com/islandimpact), and Grand Pineapple Beach properties in Jamaica, Antigua, the Turks and Caicos Islands, Saint Lucia, and the Exumas (in the Bahamas) to visit local schools to read and work with children.
- Solmar Hotels and Resorts (www.solmarfoundation.org) are located throughout Mexico, and the Solmar Foundation has a strong commitment to supporting local communities. The foundation invites guests to bring items that are needed by schools and orphanages in Mexico, including classroom supplies, toys, coloring books, stickers, and gently used clothing for women and babies. Donations can be

given to your hotel's office. Visitors to the Los Cabos location are also invited to visit one of several organizations supported by the foundation, including a shelter, nursing home, and orphanage.

- Grace Bay Resorts in the Turks and Caicos Islands (https://gracebayresorts.com) has several social-impact programs, including supporting schools, and provides a variety of volunteer opportunities for guests.

- Andaz Papagayo Costa Rica (https://papagayo.andaz.hyatt.com/en/hotel/home.html) has partnered with nonprofit organizations in the community to support children and families. If you have extra room in your luggage, you are invited to bring school supplies or a backpack that will be donated to a local school. If you and your children would like to visit a family or a school in the community, the Andaz will create a special program based on your needs and availability.

- Carnival Cruise Lines (https://www.carnival.com) has partnered with Fathom Travel (https://www.fathom.org) to create social-impact cruises to the Caribbean.

International Voluntourism Companies

- Global Volunteers (https://globalvolunteers.org) works with community partners to help families, groups, and individuals get involved in service programs around the globe.

- Give A Day Global (www.giveadayglobal.org) encourages you and your family to give one day of your vacation to a cause and provides the tools and resources to make the endeavor successful.

- Together for Good (https://wp.togetherforgood.org/OLD/) provides specific ideas for family-oriented service travel and occasionally coordinates group trips.

- Visit.org (https://visit.org/worldwide) is an online marketplace that offers a variety of purposeful, hands-on travel tours and workshops through hundreds of nonprofit organizations in several dozen countries. The focus is on short (half-day to one-day), affordable experiences that give back to local communities.

- Go Voluntouring (https://govoluntouring.com) is a directory for volunteering and applied-learning programs around the world. This organization vets programs to ensure quality and matches volunteers with projects that meet their interests.

- Me to We (https://www.metowe.org) offers a host of goods and services, including youth, adult, and family volunteer trips all over the world to destinations such as Ecuador, India, and Kenya. Volunteers work with locals to help end patterns of poverty through environmentally friendly development projects. Me to We has a positive youth-empowerment message and is famous for WEDAY, a daylong rock-concert-style event full of motivational speakers and performers who encourage the children to become change makers in the world. You can only earn a spot to attend WEDAY by completing service hours in your own community or participating in a service trip.

While I have listed a few resorts with robust social-impact programs, you should always inquire with the front desk of your hotel. The management teams of individual properties may create programs independently. For example, I once visited a Hyatt property and found a sign prominently displayed in the main lobby offering a family-friendly volunteer opportunity in the local community that had not been listed on the hotel's website.

Share, Reflect, and Keep It Going

A long-planned and highly anticipated family vacation should be a time for you and your children to unplug, get away from normal routines, and feel free to enjoy new adventures together. You are entitled to this carefree time. At the same time, incorporating service into travel can enhance your experience if you remain open to the opportunities that you encounter.

Simplicity is the key to serving when traveling with children. Small courtesies—reminding children to pick up after themselves or leaving a nice note along with a generous tip for a server who has been particularly attentive—will show your children that every person they meet, whether at home or on vacation, deserves attention and respect. If you can incorporate even bigger kindness activities into your travel plans, go for it. Whatever you choose, remember that you are teaching your children how to be their best selves and spread goodness wherever they may wander throughout their lives.

Here are some reflection questions to consider with your children during and after your vacation:

- What was your favorite part of our trip?
- Who were some of the special people we met on our trip? Wasn't that waitress (front-desk person, amusement-ride worker, or whoever) particularly nice to us? Didn't her kindness make our experience better?
- What are some ways we can show our gratitude to the people we meet on our next family trip?
- If you have not volunteered on vacation before: Would you like to go on a family service trip some time? If so, where would you like to go? Whom would you like to help?

SIMPLE ACTS IN ACTION: KINDNESS AFTER KATRINA

When my daughter Emi was seven years old, she asked whether our family could visit New Orleans, Louisiana. Even though it had been two years since Hurricane Katrina had devastated the city, she remembered upsetting media images of the terrible damage the storm had caused. She also knew that people were still struggling to recover, and she wanted to do something to help. I knew it would be difficult to find volunteer opportunities that would welcome a young child, but our family traveled to New Orleans and was lucky enough to connect with several impressive nonprofits. We worked with other families to sort and package food at Second Harvest, the largest food-recovery organization in New Orleans. We visited a women's-and-children's shelter, which had opened in response to the storm, where we worked in the garden with the children. As we explored the historic city, experiencing the music and food, we interacted with people who had survived the flood and were anxious to tell their stories. We were able to help, learn, and enjoy our time as a family and with the survivors, creating many warm memories.

The trip made a tremendous impact on Emi. She never forgot the shelter we visited, and we have continued to support it in a variety of ways. Years later, Emi decided to ask for donations to the shelter in lieu of gifts for her bat mitzvah celebration. There's no question that answering a child's call to service and allowing the child to drive the effort creates a lifelong sense of accomplishment and ignites a passion for helping others.

CHAPTER **SEVEN**
Creating Family Traditions Around Service

"At the heart of every family tradition is a meaningful experience."
—Unknown

It's hard to stay connected in a meaningful way when our schedules are so hectic and our eyes are constantly drawn to devices. Carving out time for family service is a good way to unplug and spend time together, talking about things that matter and living our values. Developing family traditions around service can ensure that you will always make the time to practice kindness.

Meg Cox, author of *The Book of New Family Traditions*, suggests that repeated family rituals create heightened attentiveness, meaning that children will actually listen and understand the purpose of your actions. Traditions add something extra that lifts an occasion above the ordinary, making it special. This assertion is supported by what Ellen Galinsky, researcher and author of *Ask the Children: What America's Children Really Think About Working Parents*, found when she surveyed children about what they would remember from childhood. Consistently, the children responded that they would remember family rituals—not onetime big events but repetitions of a treasured experience.

Of course, your traditions around service will be unique to your family, incorporating your interests, passions, religious beliefs, and values. They might develop from holiday rituals or a project you try once and decide to revisit regularly. The options are endless, and they need not overwhelm your schedule. A few treasured traditions scattered throughout your calendar will ensure that children look forward to and recognize the special qualities of a particular day or time of year.

It may feel daunting to try to start something special enough to become a beloved lifelong practice. If you don't know where to begin, use the changes of seasons as your guide. Spring is a perfect time to get outdoors with children and help care for the earth. The end of summer and beginning of fall signal the start of a new school year, a time when you hang up a new calendar full of service-learning opportunities. End-of-year celebrations, including Thanksgiving and the December holidays, offer limitless opportunities to express gratitude, help those in need, and rededicate your family to doing more service in the new year. Here are a few suggested traditions for each season to help you get started.

Service Ideas for Spring

Plant Flowers or a Garden

Gardening is a popular spring pastime and provides a chance to brighten someone's day. Even young children can help to dig holes, insert and cover up seeds, and water plants. Make a tradition of planning an afternoon of weeding, mulching, and planting for a neighbor who is unable to do so. As mentioned in chapter 1, many urban areas sponsor community gardens where residents volunteer to help with maintenance and harvesting. If you are lucky enough to have a community garden nearby, volunteer to plant flowers on the perimeters of the vegetable beds to create a beautiful oasis in the neighborhood. Being a part of this community effort is also a wonderful way to get to know people you might not otherwise have an opportunity to meet.

Participate in an Athletic Event for Charity

Identify a cause that matters to your family, and participate in a related walkathon, fun run, baseball game, or other athletic event in your community. For example, it seems that every month of the year is dedicated to raising awareness about a different health challenge—Alzheimer's, autism, Parkinson's, different types of cancer, and so on—and fund-raising athletic events to support patients and families are common, bringing hope to people dealing with challenging circumstances. Children of all ages are often welcome at these upbeat occasions. Other athletic events raise awareness about and funds for addressing social issues, such as human trafficking or recent natural disasters. Sometimes these events are simply community-building opportunities that incorporate charitable elements. For example, a 5K run/walk/ride event to get everyone out in the warm spring weather might raise funds for charity.

Spring Cleaning

The start of spring is a great time to work with children to clean out toy chests and closets and to donate gently used items. Second Chance Toys (www.secondchancetoys. org) accepts donations of gently used plastic toys. The toys are refurbished and given a second life in the hands of children living in poverty, a practice that also keeps toys out of landfills. Likewise, Goodwill (www.goodwill.org) operates donation centers and freestanding bins across the United States and happily accepts clothing, shoes, toys, books, and home items.

Last Day of School

The end of the school year is a transitional time when children bring home lots of books, supplies, and piles of artwork. It is also a great time to donate any books that your children have outgrown. Book donations are typically accepted at hospitals, libraries, underresourced public schools, the Ronald McDonald House (https://www.rmhc.org), Goodwill, foster-care agencies, and other nonprofits serving children in need. To avoid being overwhelmed with papers, sit with your children and sort through artwork and select a few special pieces to keep or frame. Consider putting the rest together and sending them to Color A Smile (https://colorasmileorg.presencehost.net/), or deliver a package of colorful creations to your local senior center, nursing home, or assisted-living center.

Service Ideas for Summer

Participate in a Backpack Drive

A backpack drive needs to begin early in the summer to be sure you have time to collect materials, fill backpacks, and get them delivered to recipient agencies. Agencies will need to receive them by mid-August so that they can be distributed to children in need prior to the start of school. This tradition of service will give your family the satisfaction of helping children who don't have many resources, allowing them to start a new school year with confidence and dignity.

- Local community organizations, such as Family Giving Tree (https://familygivingtree.org/) in the Bay Area of California, A Precious Child (https://apreciouschild.org/) in Colorado, Backpack Beginnings (https://backpackbeginnings.org/) in North Carolina, or Project Backpack through the Center for Family Services (https://www.centerffs.org/get-involved/campaigns/project-backpack) in New Jersey, help provide backpacks, school supplies, or both to children in need. An internet search using the terms "backpack donations" or "donating school supplies" can uncover similar opportunities in your area.
- If you live in one of the regions in the following list, consider supporting Operation Backpack (https://www.voa.org/operation-backpack), which provides backpacks full of school supplies to children who are homeless or from underresourced communities. Information and shopping lists can be found online to help you coordinate a backpack drive, or you can simply add a few extra

items to your own shopping cart. Donations are often collected at pharmacies, banks, or FedEx stores. Operation Backpack covers these regions:

East Coast

- New York City
- Washington, DC
- Boston
- Pennsylvania

South

- Mobile, Alabama

Midwest

- Ohio
- Chicago
- Indiana
- Michigan

West Coast

- California (Bay Area and Sacramento)
- Nevada (Reno and Sparks)

- Cradles to Crayons (https://www.cradlestocrayons.org) collects items for children in need and has locations in Chicago, Boston, and Philadelphia, as well as partnerships with other organizations across the country.
- The Kids in Need Foundation (https://www.kinf.org) sponsors the nationwide "School Ready Supplies" program to provide supplies to students and teachers through a nationwide network of resource centers. Explore the Kids in Need Foundation website to learn more about hosting a collection drive.
- Family-to-Family (https://www.family-to-family.org) provides detailed instructions for a variety of summer service projects, including a backpack drive.
- Daymaker (https://www.daymaker.com) is a child-to-child platform where your family can search a database of children who need help in your area. You can purchase specific back-to-school items from a wish list and track the items as they are shipped and delivered to the recipient.

Host a Lemonade Stand for Charity

I can never pass a lemonade stand without stopping. There's something about the little cups and the too-sweet drink that pulls me in and makes me want to support the child behind the table. Hosting a lemonade stand for charity is a fun way to spend a summer day with children and teaches many lessons—from making change to providing good customer service with a smile and a thank you. It's also a perfect opportunity for children to raise awareness and money for a cause they care about. Here are a few suggestions to get you started:

- Talk to children in advance about the cause or organization they would like to support with the proceeds of their stand. If they don't know of a specific organization but have an idea of the cause (for example, they want to help animals), take a little time to search online for a local or national organization to which you can donate the proceeds.

- Children can make a sign describing the organization their lemonade stand is supporting. The sign can include images from the organization's website or personal photos of your family volunteering together. The more personal the issue, the better, as children will connect with it and hopefully will feel comfortable sharing information about it with their customers.

- Decorate a small collection box and place it at the front of the table for additional donations. People will often tell children to keep the change for a good cause.

- If you hold your lemonade stand in late summer (September is Childhood Cancer Awareness Month), consider supporting Alex's Lemonade Stand Foundation (https://www.alexslemonade.org), which raises money for pediatric cancer research. The foundation provides resources such as a how-to video and printables to customize your lemonade stand and make it a success.

- When sending or delivering your children's lemonade-stand donation to the charity, make sure to include a note from your children and a picture of them working at the lemonade stand (if you feel comfortable doing so). You are almost certain to receive a positive, personal response from the organization, and your children can feel the pride of accomplishment and of being acknowledged. Remind them, though, that the true reward is in helping, not in being recognized.

Share the Joy of Summer Camp

Summer day and sleep-away camps are filled with physical activity, artistic expression, friendships, fun, and team building. For many children who come from underresourced communities or who are experiencing health challenges in their families, summer camps provide a respite from difficult circumstances and a chance to enjoy a safe and nurturing environment. There are many ways your family can support local and national camps serving children with a variety of needs.

- Explore camps hosted by your local YMCA or YWCA, Big Brothers Big Sisters chapter, community recreation center, or other youth organization. For example, New York is home to the Fresh Air Fund (www.freshair.org), which provides summer camps and host-family programs for inner-city children. Children can attend a week of traditional sleep-away camp outside of the city, or they can request to be matched with a volunteer family, who will host a child for a week in their suburban or vacation home. My family has hosted a Fresh Air Fund child several times, and it is always a fun and rewarding experience. In addition to giving financial donations, your family may be able to volunteer at a camp, host a child, donate equipment, or provide transportation or other support.

- SCOPE USA (http://scopeusa.org) provides life-changing summer-camp experiences for children from underserved communities. The organization raises funds and creates scholarships at participating camps, and campers must commit to stay in school in order to be able to return to camp the following summer. Project ideas and additional information can be found on SCOPE's website.

- Camp Kesem (http://campkesem.org) provides a camp experience for children whose parents have been diagnosed with cancer. The organization encourages families and individuals to host fund-raisers to #GiveKidsKesem.

Show Gratitude for Military, Veterans, and First Responders

There are opportunities throughout the year to honor and show appreciation for active-duty military, veterans, first responders, and military families, but patriotic summer holidays can be particularly meaningful times for these types of projects. Every child should understand and appreciate the sacrifices of the people, often putting their own safety at risk, who work to keep us safe and help us in emergencies. If members of your family are veterans or are currently serving in the military or working as first responders, your children will immediately connect with these projects and find them meaningful. Here are a few ways you can show your support and gratitude:

- Plan a visit to your local Veterans of Foreign Wars (VFW) post or Veterans Administration hospital or nursing home, and deliver cards, baked goods, books, and smiles.

- Bake muffins or cookies, and deliver them to the local firehouse or police precinct. Children can create colorful cards or drawings to include in the package.

- Explore one of the many nonprofits that support our active-duty military and veterans. For a comprehensive listing of these organizations, explore the Operation We Are Here website (www.operationwearehere.org).

- Make or collect items to put in military care packages. The website of the military-support organization Operation Gratitude (https://www.operationgratitude.com/express-your-thanks) provides some ideas:
  - Host a collection drive for small plush toys, which are a welcome addition to care packages and provide comfort to soldiers serving far from home.
  - Create care kits or host a care-kit assembly party. Care kits consist of seven to ten personal items, including socks, hand sanitizer, mouthwash, tissue packs, lip balm, toiletries, and batteries.
  - Start a Cents for Service coin collection to help Operation Gratitude raise the funds necessary to send care packages overseas.

- Create Cool Ties for soldiers serving in hot climates. Cool Ties can be soaked with cold water and worn around the neck or as headbands on hot days. Directions are available on the website.
- Say thanks with cards and letters. The website provides helpful tips about appropriate things to write.
- If you have a child who loves to knit or crochet, even if he is just learning, try making hats and scarves for soldiers. The website provides instructions about materials and colors to use.
- Purchase paracord, and create survival bracelets. The website provides a how-to video. As this activity involves braiding, it works best for older children.

Service Ideas for Fall

Rake Leaves

Autumn is a fantastic time for children to play outside, and if you live in a climate where trees shed their leaves, identify an elderly or ill neighbor whose yard could use raking. If children are very young, adults can rake and children can help with the bagging process. Children can collect a few particularly colorful leaves to use in arts-and-crafts kindness projects once they go back inside. For example, you can press a few leaves and some crayon shavings between two sheets of wax paper. Cover the wax-paper "sandwich" with a dish towel, and use an iron (adult only) on a low setting to melt the crayon shavings and adhere the sheets together, creating a colorful piece of art. Children can also make simple leaf rubbings with white paper and the side of a crayon. Encourage children to take some of their art over to the neighbor whose yard you raked to share the beauty of your neighborhood foliage.

Share the Sweetness of Halloween

Halloween is one of the happiest days of the year for children. What could be better than dressing up and collecting (and eating) candy? It is a totally child-centric holiday, making it a perfect opportunity to incorporate family giving traditions. Here are some ideas for sharing the sweetness.

Costume Collection

During late September and early October, sort through your dress-up box for outgrown costumes, and collect other gently used costumes from friends, family, and classmates. You can donate them to a social-service agency working with children in your community. If you have difficulty finding a place to donate costumes, contact 'WeenDream (www.weendream.org), a nonprofit that gives costumes to children all over the country who are facing challenges from natural disasters to disabilities to poverty.

Trick-or-Treat for UNICEF

Order a collection box or download printables and instructions from the UNICEF website (https://www.unicefusa.org/trick-or-treat) so that your children can collect coins for humanitarian causes while trick-or-treating. This initiative has helped to raise more than $175 million since it began.

Operation Gratitude Candy Give-Back Program

After children have returned home with bulging bags of candy, sort through "extra" candy together and create a pile for donation to the Candy Give-Back program sponsored by Operation Gratitude (https://www.operationgratitude.com), a nonprofit that supports active-duty military and veterans. Detailed instructions about safely shipping candy can be found on the website, as well as a donation form that must be included with your package. It's always a nice idea to include letters of encouragement and thanks, along with individually wrapped toothbrushes, dental floss, and toothpaste in your shipment. Your local pediatric dental practice may have its own candy give-back program, encouraging children to trade leftover candy for toothbrushes and other prizes during office visits.

Thanksgiving: The Perfect Holiday for Gratitude and Service

Thanksgiving is a tradition-filled day that kicks off the end-of-year holiday season of shopping, decorating, exchanging gifts, and, hopefully, charitable giving. No matter how your family honors Thanksgiving, it is full of opportunities to create new family traditions that help children understand how lucky they are to have the comforts of home, food, and family and that teach family members to express gratitude for all of the goodness in their lives.

Volunteering with your children at an organization that feeds the hungry is an excellent way to show gratitude on or near a day of feasting. Understandably, it might be difficult to find time away from grocery shopping, cooking, and baking, and in some cases, young children are not allowed to assist in food preparation. However, most organizations that work to fight hunger begin preparations for Thanksgiving well in advance of the holiday and may offer other roles for children, such as stocking shelves or filling bags with donated groceries. For many of these organizations, this is the busiest time of the year, when they feed the most people and provide support for additional families who are not regular clients but who don't have the resources to make a special Thanksgiving feast. There is great need, and there are many ways your family can help, even if you only have a little time to spare. If you are unfamiliar with the location of a local food pantry, food-delivery organization, or soup kitchen, these online resources can help you find one:

- Feeding America (www.feedingamerica.org/find-your-local-foodbank)
- Food Pantries (https://www.foodpantries.org)

- Ample Harvest (http://ampleharvest.org/donate-food)
- Meals on Wheels (https://www.mealsonwheelsamerica.org/signup/find-programs)

Also try reaching out to houses of worship and other faith-based organizations, as they frequently help to feed the hungry at Thanksgiving. Once you've identified an appropriate organization to help, inquire about what kinds of assistance are needed around Thanksgiving. Here are some ways your family can make a difference:

- During the month of November, work with your children to organize a canned-food drive in your neighborhood; with a Girl or Boy Scout troop; or in your apartment building, school, or house of worship. Collect specific requested Thanksgiving foods.
- Donate frozen turkeys to your local food pantry, or contribute grocery-store gift cards.
- Ask whether you and your family can bake and donate pies or other desserts.
- In the weeks leading up to Thanksgiving, encourage children to create cards or decorate place mats, shopping bags, or boxes to be used or included in Thanksgiving deliveries.

At your own Thanksgiving table with family and friends, be sure to include time for reflection about gratitude and kindness. Take a moment during the meal to allow each person to mention a specific thing for which he or she is grateful. Ask everyone to write down his words of gratitude on a colorful slip of paper (along with his name and the date) and add them to a gratitude jar. The jar can be a centerpiece of your Thanksgiving table each year. Every few years, pull a few slips of paper out of the jar during dinner and read them aloud. These mementos will become treasured remembrances as time goes by.

Arts-and-crafts projects that help children express gratitude and brighten the Thanksgiving dinner table are easily found online. Here are some favorites:

- Trace children's hands, and cut out the outlines to create handprint turkeys. On each "feather," children can write a person or thing for which they are grateful.
- Paper "gratitude leaves" can be hung from a stick.
- An individualized place mat for each guest can list the top ten things that the child loves or appreciates about that person.

Service Ideas for Winter

Shovel Snow

If you live in an area that experiences snowfall each year, you know how much children love to play in the snow. While being outdoors on a wintry day is full of fun activities—sledding, snowball fights, building a snowman or snow fort, making snow angels, and more—children can also be encouraged to help out with the more mundane tasks that ice and snow necessitate. Even young children can help to clear snow from walkways, paths, and porches or help to spread salt. The elderly and disabled are often forced to stay indoors when walkways and roads are snowy or icy, making even retrieving mail or a newspaper from the stoop difficult. Identify a neighbor who could use help with snow removal, and engage your children in shoveling or sweeping snow and spreading salt. Once you go back indoors to warm up and enjoy hot chocolate, children can create winter-themed arts and crafts, such as paper snowmen or scissor-cut snowflakes, for their neighbors. They can deliver these, along with some fresh-baked cookies, to brighten the day of a homebound friend.

Spread Joy during the End-of-Year Holidays

The end-of-year holiday season is ripe with opportunities to help those in need. Since your calendar is likely to be packed, try choosing just one or two special kindness activities that resonate with your family. These projects can become cherished family traditions while helping your children appreciate the gifts and treats they receive at this time of year. Here are a few ideas to consider.

"Adopt" a Family or a Child

- Family-to-Family (https://www.family-to-family.org) offers a variety of ways for your family to give back around the end-of-year holidays, including "adopting" a family, filling stockings for children in need, and donating holiday dinner baskets for hungry families. Depending on the ages and maturity levels of your children, they can even choose to give up some gifts they would have received and instead donate gifts from a wish list created by a child in need.
- Operation Christmas Spirit through Operation Help a Hero (https://www.operationhelpahero.org) enables your family to help active-duty military and their families in a variety of ways at the end-of-year holidays, including "adopting" a military family or single service member, hosting a toy drive, or donating gift cards.
- One Simple Wish (https://www.onesimplewish.org) and Daymaker (https://www.daymaker.com) are two organizations offering similar opportunities. Your family can search a database of children and purchase a specific gift from a child's wish list, tracking the gift as it is shipped and received.
- Many community nonprofits, including Catholic Charities (https://www.catholiccharitiesusa.org) and local houses of worship, offer "adopt-a-family" opportunities at the end-of-year holidays.

Visit an Elderly Neighbor and Deliver a Holiday Package

In New York City, a senior-services organization called Dorot (www.dorotusa.org) organizes Hanukkah visits to the elderly. This has become a cherished family tradition in our home, anxiously anticipated each year for one night of Hanukkah. Similar senior-focused social-service agencies likely exist in your community. You might also coordinate a visit to a local assisted-living facility or nursing home to do some caroling door to door or during a meal service. Bring holiday greeting cards or small handmade gifts to distribute to the residents during your visit.

Donate Toys or Other Gifts

- Fill Christmas stockings with toiletries, makeup, and small gifts to donate to women in domestic-violence or homeless shelters. The value of these treats for women who have been traumatized or displaced is immeasurable.

- The Marine Corps Toys for Tots Program (https://www.toysfortots.org) distributes millions of toys during the end-of-year holiday season. Collection boxes are set up in many communities, and many retailers host toy drives.

- Through Macy's Believe Campaign (https://www.macys.com/social/believe), children of all ages can download a letter-to-Santa template from the Macy's website and drop a stamped letter, addressed to Santa at the North Pole, in the Santa Mail letter box at any Macy's retail store. For each letter received, Macy's will donate one dollar to Make-A-Wish (http://wish.org), a nonprofit that grants wishes to children with life-threatening diseases.

- Participate in Operation Santa through the US Postal Service (https://about.usps.com/holidaynews/operation-santa.htm). In select locations around the United States, your family can visit a participating post office to "adopt" a letter from a child. You respond directly to the child and fulfill the wishes outlined in that child's letter to Santa.

- Join in Operation Christmas Child through Samaritan's Purse (https://www.samaritanspurse.org/what-we-do/operation-christmas-child/). In the month of November, your family can pack a shoebox full of gifts, deliver it to one of the nationwide drop- off locations, and track it through a bar code label attached to your box as it is delivered to a child in need somewhere around the world.

- Your local Ronald McDonald House (https://www.rmhc.org) will always accept donations of new toys and games, especially at the end-of-year holidays.

- In Operation Holiday Joy through the YMCA (www.asymca.org/operation-holiday-joy), financial donations are used to purchase Thanksgiving baskets and holiday gifts for military families.

- St. Jude Children's Research Hospital (https://www.stjude.org) always accepts donations of new toys, which can be sent to the hospital in Memphis, Tennessee.

Donate to a Coat Drive

If you live in a cold climate, winter is a good time to sort through gently used, outgrown coats, hats, scarves, and gloves and donate them to one of the many organizations fighting poverty and helping the homeless in your community.

- One Warm Coat (https://www.onewarmcoat.org) is a national nonprofit supporting coat drives across the nation. The website provides all of the materials and information you need to host your own coat drive or to help you find an existing coat drive in your area.

- Operation Warm (https://www.operationwarm.org) provides brand-new coats for children in need across the United States. You can support this important work with a financial donation or a fund-raising campaign.
- Other regional nonprofits, such as Give a Kid a Coat (https://www.giveakidacoat. org), New York Cares Coat Drive (https://www.newyorkcares.org/coat-drive), and Jersey Cares (https://www.jerseycares.org/The_Jersey_Cares_Coat_Drive) provide coat-drive opportunities. A quick online search for your area will likely uncover similar efforts.

Make Blankets

This is a great project for anytime during the winter months. It is particularly appropriate for the third Saturday in February, designated as Make a Blanket Day by Project Linus (https://www.projectlinus.org/mabd). Project Linus provides handmade blankets and afghans to children who are seriously ill, traumatized, or otherwise in need. Make a Blanket Day was organized to promote Project Linus's mission and to encourage families to make financial donations or create blankets for donation. Binky Patrol (https://www. binkypatrol.org) is a similar organization that encourages individuals and groups to organize "bink-a-thons," events to make blankets for children in need across the United States. There are Binky Patrol chapters in almost every state. Most young children have special blankets or stuffed toys that bring them comfort, so it's easy to engage your children in a conversation about the love we can spread to children in need by giving them blankets of their own. See "Pajama Party or Sleepover" on page 25 for detailed instructions for making simple fleece blankets.

Service Ideas for Religious and Cultural Celebrations

Your family may already have some service traditions associated with your own religious and cultural holidays or observances. These meaningful times are the perfect opportunity to give back to your community. Of course, no single book can cover every cultural or religious observance, so a few sample events are included here. Try some of these ideas to commemorate these special days (and others like them) with service and kindness.

Day of the Big Game

Each year, sports fans worldwide assemble around their TVs to watch playoff and championship matches. In the United States, for example, professional football's culminating game occurs each year in late January or early February, and college-basketball playoffs consume much of March. These "holidays" bring friends and families together for large parties to eat, socialize, and watch the games, and these occasions provide a perfect opportunity to allow your children to lead a service component of the festivities. Since special game-day food is a major element of these events, ask party guests to bring donations for a local food pantry, or request donations of gently used sports equipment for a local youth-service organization. Children who tire of watching the game can create cards for food-pantry clients or write letters of support and gratitude for active-duty military members, which are accepted by organizations such as Operation Gratitude (https://www.operationgratitude.com), Operation Help a Hero (https://www.operationhelpahero.org), or Soldiers' Angels (https://soldiersangels. org). Families can also initiate fund-raising activities tied to the elements of the game. Instead of adults betting on the coin toss or on which team will score first, children can encourage donations to a favorite charity for each point scored.

Lunar New Year

Much of the world celebrates the new calendar year on January 1, but some nations, including China, Korea, and Vietnam, also commemorate the lunar new year later in the winter. Traditionally, these celebrations include eating special foods, giving gifts or "lucky" money, sharing holiday greetings, visiting friends and family, and setting off fireworks. According to Wes Radez of the website Chinese American Family, there are many ways to engage children in observing the lunar new year, and many of these traditions inherently include service and generosity. The ritual of preparing the home by sweeping away bad luck and making the house ready to receive good luck is a perfect way to remind children that service begins at home. You might also offer to assist an elderly or ill family member or neighbor with the physically challenging task of cleaning the house in preparation for the new year. Gifts of lucky money, presented in red envelopes, are traditionally given to children but can also be distributed to employees and friends. These envelopes need not contain large amounts of money—the symbolism of spreading luck and joy in the red envelope is what is most important—and children can help prepare and distribute these gifts to friends, employees, and service professionals who help your family all year long. The general mood of the lunar new year is one of goodwill. Celebrants should interact with others in a positive manner and avoid quarrels. The lunar new year provides another opportunity to talk to children about approaching a new season with a clean slate and making all of our interactions with others positive, helpful, and kind.

Carnival and Mardi Gras

These celebrations traditionally precede the more restrained Christian observance of Lent. Carnival and Mardi Gras are typically marked by merrymaking, such as eating, drinking, costume balls, and parades. Children can be encouraged to partake in the joy of the holiday by creating colorful masks and bags of sweets tied up with colorful beads and bringing them to a local nursing home or senior center to spread some joy. Your family can also create activity kits for hospitalized children or your local Ronald

McDonald House (https://www.rmhc.org). Fill a ziplock bag with a plain white mask (you can find blank patterns online), colorful beads, markers, sticker jewels, and an instruction sheet.

If your family enjoys baking together, make a brightly decorated king cake to share with neighbors and friends. After baking the cake but before frosting it, insert a tiny plastic baby doll somewhere in the cake. Frost the cake in purple, green, and yellow icing, then cut the cake into slices and deliver them to neighbors. Add a note explaining that the person who finds the baby is sure to experience luck and prosperity in the coming year.

Lent, Easter, and Passover

The Christian observances of Lent and Easter and the Jewish holiday of Passover all arrive in spring. During the forty-day period of Lent, many Christians fast or give up luxuries and use their time and resources to help others. Lent culminates with the Easter celebration, a time when many Christians donate to charities or volunteer. During Passover, most Jewish families host a Seder meal and often invite strangers or acquaintances who are celebrating alone to join them. Local houses of worship frequently offer opportunities to honor these observances by engaging in family service. Other organizations that might sponsor service projects at these times include Catholic Charities (https://www.catholiccharitiesusa.org), the Jewish Federations of North America (https://www.jewishfederations.org), Catholic Relief Services (https://www.crs. org/), Samaritan's Purse (https://www.samaritanspurse.org), and World Vision (https:// www.worldvision.org).

Holi

According to reporter Manveena Suri of CNN, this Hindu festival commemorates the beginning of spring and good defeating evil. It is well-known for the tradition of tossing colored water and powder on family and friends. It is a time of brotherhood and closeness, when friends, families, and communities get together without regard for ethnic differences. Many people who observe Holi visit with friends after the colorful revelry and exchange sweets as a symbol of joy and friendship. Children can help to prepare traditional gifts such Holi color packs; bags of dried fruits or chocolates; decorative items for the home, such as handmade floral baskets or wall hangings; or simple handmade greeting cards expressing love and admiration for the recipients. Engaging children in the activity of creating or preparing gifts for others is a great way to foster generosity and instill the joy of gift giving.

Purim

This festival, commemorating the Jews' triumph over persecution and imminent destruction, falls during late winter or early spring. The Purim tradition of giving baskets of treats to neighbors and friends is an opportunity for families to practice generosity and spread kindness. In our family, we create rainbow-colored *hamentaschen* (triangular fruit- or chocolate-filled cookies) and give plates to friends and neighbors.

Ramadan

This Muslim holy month, whose timing varies from year to year, is marked by daily fasting from dawn to dusk. According to Manal Ibham and the Muslim Aid website, Muslims frequently use this period to give charitable donations and perform acts of kindness. Many mosques and Muslim charities sponsor donation drives and host volunteer events during Ramadan.

Diwali and Sukkot

According to Tarandip Kaur and Encyclopedia Britannica, Diwali—the festival of lights—is celebrated by Hindus each fall. A time of starting again, it commemorates important events in the lives of certain gods and good overcoming evil. Feasts, special ceremonies, and the lighting of thousands of small lamps are all significant traditions. In the Hindu faith, darkness represents ignorance, so the lighting of lanterns at Diwali represents knowledge and the destruction of negative forces. It is a joyful celebration of light and color, and it is customary for celebrants to exchange gifts and sweets with loved ones and friends as an expression of love and gratitude. Children can create handmade gifts and cards for family and friends, and it is especially important to include messages of appreciation and respect. Children can also participate in creating colorful *rangoli*—geometric designs drawn on the floor of the entryway of a home—that symbolize warm welcome and good luck.

At around the same time of year, the Jewish festival of Sukkot celebrates the gathering of the harvest. Many families build a foliage-covered shelter outside and invite friends to eat a festive meal together in it. As with other Jewish holidays, it is customary to invite strangers, those who are new to the community, or those who are far from home to share in family gatherings. Extending your hospitality and sharing a warm and festive meal with those who might not have a place to celebrate is a particularly meaningful way to spread the joy of the holiday.

Kwanzaa

According to Dr. Maulana Karenga (the founder of this holiday) and The Official Kwanzaa Website, Kwanzaa is observed by people of African heritage around the world from December 26 through January 1 to honor African culture and values. As the United States and other countries become more ethnically and racially diverse, families of all backgrounds are becoming more engaged in observing and honoring the principles of Kwanzaa: unity, self-determination, collective work and responsibility, cooperative economics, purpose, creativity, and faith. Families who do not share African heritage should be sensitive to and respectful of the true meaning of the holiday—that those of African ancestry observe the seven days of Kwanzaa to remember and honor their roots and to foster unity and create community with other people of African heritage. However, any family can use the holiday as an opportunity to learn about its special meaning and to spread kindness and goodwill. Specifically, Amanda Rock of Verywell Family highlights the importance of creativity as part of this celebration, especially on the day of the *Karamu* feast (typically December 31). Children can be encouraged to share expressions of creativity, such as singing, for friends and family members to enjoy. They can also make signs, cards, or other crafts and can present them to loved ones on the last day of Kwanzaa.

End-of-Year "Giving" Holidays

Many religious and cultural observances and holidays take place in the period of November through January and incorporate the giving of gifts. These special occasions include Hanukkah, Saint Nicholas's Day, Christmas, Three Kings' Day, and others. There is perhaps no better time of year to cultivate family traditions around service than during these giving-focused events. In addition to sharing our abundance with those in need through gift giving, these holidays are perfect times for your family to engage in hands-on service to create joy in myriad ways. Any social-service agency serving children and families will need some kind of assistance at this time of year, as budgets begin to run out and these organizations have their hands full attempting to make the holidays special for those who are marginalized. Your family can find meaningful volunteer opportunities preparing or serving meals in soup kitchens, food pantries, or meal-delivery programs. You might also be able to help with holiday parties and visits from Santa at foster-care agencies, domestic-violence and homeless shelters, social-service agencies serving children who have disabilities or have experienced trauma, or senior centers.

Share, Reflect, and Keep It Going

I hope that this book has been filled with fun, simple, and unique ideas for incorporating acts of kindness into busy family schedules. The one overarching principle has been that service is powerful and transformative when you find the time to make it a regular part of your family's life.

In fact, the keys to successful family service projects are also the keys to creating lasting family traditions. When you find a purpose for your projects by addressing issues you care about as a family, you build the foundation for ongoing practices. Keeping it simple and creative ensures that a tradition is easy to continue but does not become stale over time. Making it fun for all ages enables you to keep the tradition going for years to come. As you develop and maintain relationships with the people, organizations, and communities you assist, your children will form caring connections that increase their desire to continue the tradition. And when you find time for reflection and ongoing effort, your children will come to understand how traditions of kindness bless both those who are served and those who serve. In short, by developing family service traditions, you and your children will reap the benefits now and over time.

Here are some reflection questions to consider as you build your family's traditions of kindness:

- Before you begin, consider creating a family mission statement. What are your family values? What are the issues you each care about? How can you make an impact on those issues?
- What does your family enjoy doing together? What are your favorite activities in each season? Is there a way to incorporate service into something you are already doing, or is there a small change you can make to begin to shift the focus to the outside world and those in need around you?

SIMPLE ACTS IN ACTION: HANUKKAH FRIENDS

My family's favorite holiday tradition is our annual Hanukkah visit through Dorot (www.dorotusa.org), a social-service agency supporting the elderly in Manhattan. Dorot coordinates home visits with seniors during all major Jewish holidays. Families register for the program and receive training in advance. Each family is assigned one senior (or a couple) to visit on a specific night. Dorot provides a bag of traditional treats for the visiting family to bring so that they don't arrive empty-handed. Hanukkah bags, for example, might contain cookies; a dreidel, so the children and the seniors can play together; a small menorah, candles, and matches; and a handmade holiday card. I signed up for our first Hanukkah visit when I was pregnant with my younger daughter, Alaina, and we have been participating ever since.

That first year, my family was matched with an elderly couple whom I'll call Danek and Marta, who were both Holocaust survivors. Danek had been incapacitated by a stroke but was always present for our visits, sitting in his recliner and observing the gathering. Marta was spry and sweet, fussing over us in her finest fluffy pink sweater. With the help of an aide, she always prepared mini latkes and honey cake for our visit. Danek and Marta had a cat named Sylvester, and my children enjoyed playing with him. We would light the candles of the menorah, play dreidel, and sing songs together. It was always a delightful visit, full of smiles and warmth, and we requested to visit the couple year after year. The best feeling in the world was having my children ask me each Hanukkah, "What night are we doing our Dorot visit?"

After eight or nine years, Marta suffered a fall and a broken hip. She was shaky and using a walker that Hanukkah, but we still had a wonderful time. The following year, she passed away, and Dorot informed us that Danek was no longer requesting visits.

My family now visits other seniors on our Dorot outings, different people each year. All are lovely, but we still talk about Danek and Marta and remember them fondly. Connecting with them and developing a bond over several years created a meaningful tradition around the holiday season for my family and continues to inspire our kindness practice.

RESOURCE **GUIDE**

There are many excellent organizations and websites promoting family volunteerism and offering tips, resources, and inspiring stories, as well as databases of volunteer opportunities that can be searched by zip code. Most of these organizations also use social media to spread the good word about service and kindness, so be sure to follow the programs that resonate with you and your family. Obviously, no single book can list every service organization that exists, but this resource guide should give you a good start.

Doing Good Together

Doing Good Together offers a robust website (https://www.doinggoodtogether.org) full of ideas, tools, insights, and links. It is worth exploring and checking often. Here are some of the best resources on it:

- Pick a Project—a collection of dozens of kindness projects
- Reading with Empathy—a collection of book lists organized by themes such as gratitude, mindfulness, healing the world, bullying, diversity, and citizenship
- Start Kind Conversations—a collection of tips and sample questions to spark meaningful conversations with your children
- Teach Kindness—practical tips on topics like diversity, gratitude, and expanding emotional intelligence
- A Family Service-Fair Manual (for purchase and download)—a resource to help your school or organization host a successful family-service fair
- Service and Smiles—free weekly kindness tips for your school or club newsletter
- A full archive of Doing Good Together newsletters and blog posts
- Free printables, including "kindness challenge" sheets
- A "shop kind" online store

National Organizations and Useful Websites

- The Nature Conservancy—https://www.nature.org/en-us/
- Start A Snowball—http://startasnowball.com/
- Bucket Fillers—http://www.bucketfillers101.com/
- Pennies of Time—http://penniesoftime.com/
- Family-to-Family—https://www.family-to-family.org/
- Volunteers of America—https://www.voa.org/ (search for local chapters)
- Create the Good—http://www.createthegood.org/
- Idealist—https://www.idealist.org/en/?type=JOB (check "appropriate for families" filter)

- Volunteer Match—https://www.volunteermatch.org/ (check "great for kids" filter)
- Just Serve—https://www.justserve.org/ (check "suitable for all ages" filter under "other options")
- GenerationON—https://www.generationON.org/
- Points of Light Foundation—http://www.pointsoflight.org/
- Points of Light HandsOn Network—http://www.pointsoflight.org/handsonnetwork
- United Way—https://www.unitedway.org/
- Cradles to Crayons—https://www.cradlestocrayons.org/
- Thankful—https://www.thankful.org/
- DoSomething.org—https://www.dosomething.org/us
- Project Sunshine—https://projectsunshine.org/
- Inspired2C—http://www.inspired2c.org/
- Choose Kindness—https://www.kindness.org/
- Learning to Give—https://www.learningtogive.org/
- The Kindness Evolution—www.kindnessevolution.org
- Kindness Matters—https://kindness-matters.org/
- Strength Behind Stars—https://strengthbehindstars.org/
- World Kindness Movement—http://www.theworldkindnessmovement.org/
- The Joy Team—http://thejoyteam.org/
- Spread Kindness—http://www. spreadkindness.org/
- Charter for Compassion—https://charterforcompassion.org/
- The Great Kindness Challenge—https://thegreatkindnesschallenge.com/
- VolunTEEN Nation—http://volunteennation.org/
- Give Gab—https://www.givegab.com/
- Ronald McDonald House—https://www.rmhc.org/
- Big Brothers Big Sisters of America—http://www.bbbs.org/
- Catholic Charities USA—https://www.catholiccharitiesusa.org/
- Samaritans Purse—https://www.samaritanspurse.org/
- All Hands and Hearts—https://www.allhandsandhearts.org/
- Corporation for National and Community Service (Americorps)— http://www. nationalservice.gov/programs/americorps

Kindness State by State

Online searches for your specific town or region will uncover organizations that can connect you to family-friendly volunteer opportunities in your area. While there are many grassroots organizations focused on volunteerism around the United States, several of the organizations listed below are powered by national nonprofits such as the United Way, Volunteer Match, or the Hands-On Network (an affiliate of the Points of

Light Foundation). Connecting with locally managed nonprofits, some examples of which are listed below, will likely present additional meaningful opportunities for your family.

Alabama

HandsOn River Region—http://www.handsonriverregion.org/

Children's of Alabama—https://www.childrensal.org/

HandsOn Birmingham—https://www.handsonbirmingham.org/

Alabama Governor's Office of Volunteer Services—https://www.servealabama.gov/

Alaska

Stone Soup Group—https://www.stonesoupgroup.org/

Food Bank Alaska—http://www.foodbankofalaska.org/

The Alaska Center—https://akcenter.org/

Arizona

Families Giving Back—http://www.familiesgivingback.org/site/

HandsOn Greater Phoenix—https://www.handsonphoenix.org/

Arizona Helping Hands, Inc.—https://www.azhelpinghands.org/

City of Tempe Volunteer Program—https://www.tempe.gov/city-hall/community-services/volunteer

Keep Phoenix Beautiful—http://www.kpbvolunteers.org/

Valley of the Sun United Way—https://vsuw.org/

Arkansas

Volunteer AR—https://www.volunteerar.org/

Arkansas Dream Center—https://ardreamcenter.tv/

Arkansas Department of Human Services—https://humanservices.arkansas.gov/

Arkansas Children's—https://www.archildrens.org/

California

Doing Good Together (Silicon Valley)—https://www.doinggoodtogether.org/family-volunteering-silicon-valley

Give Together—http://www.givegrow.org/

Simple Acts of Care and Kindness—http://www.simpleacts.org/

OneOC—http://www.oneoc.org/

Family Giving Tree—https://familygivingtree.org/

Project Giving Kids—https://www.projectgivingkids.org/

Together We Rise—https://www.togetherwerise.org/

Baby2Baby—http://baby2baby.org/

Colorado

Kids' Compassion Project—https://www.kidscompassionproject.org/

A Precious Child—https://apreciouschild.org/

Bessie's Hope—https://www.bessieshope.org/

Connecticut

Volunteer CT—http://www.volunteerct.org/

Connecticut Humane Society—http://www.cthumane.org/

Tails of Courage—https://tailsofcourage.org/

Riverfront Recapture—http://www.riverfront.org/

Delaware

Volunteer Delaware—https://www.volunteerdelaware.org/

Ronald McDonald House of Delaware—https://rmhde.org/

Food Bank Delaware—https://www.fbd.org/

Florida

Volunteer Florida—https://www.volunteerflorida.org/

HandsOn Broward—https://www.handsonbroward.org/

Fun 4 Orlando Kids—http://fun4orlandokids.com/

Miami Diaper Bank—http://www.miamidiaperbank.com/

Georgia

Pebble Tossers—https://www.pebbletossers.org/

Nicholas House—https://nicholashouse.org/

Meals by Grace—https://mealsbygrace.org/

Helping Mamas—https://www.helpingmamas.org/

Trees Atlanta—https://treesatlanta.org/

Fur Kids—https://furkids.org/

Hawaii

Project Hawaii, Inc.—https://www.helpthehomelesskeiki.org/

Malama Na Honu—http://www.malamanahonu.org/

Lanakila Meals on Wheels—https://www.lanakilapacific.org/senior-services/meals-on-wheels/

Lunalilo Home—http://lunalilo.org/

Malama Maunalua—http://www.malamamaunalua.org/

Hawaiian Humane Society—https://www.hawaiianhumane.org/

Idaho

Idaho CareLine—https://211.idaho.gov/default.aspx

The Idaho Food Bank—https://idahofoodbank.org/

Boise Rescue Mission Ministries—https://boiserm.org/

Boise Bicycle Project—http://www.boisebicycleproject.org/

Illinois

The Honeycomb Project—http://thehoneycombproject.org/

Chicago Cares—http://chicagocares.force.com/

Books First Chicago—https://www.booksfirstchicago.org/

Lakeview Pantry—https://www.lakeviewpantry.org/

Share Our Space—https://shareourspace.org/

Indiana

IndyHub—https://indyhub.org/

CHEER Committee at Mid-North Food Pantry—http://www.midnorthfoodpantry.org/i-want-to-help/cheer-committee/

Conner Prairie—http://www.connerprairie.org/

Art With a Heart—http://artwithaheart.us/

Good Samaritan Network—https://www.gsnlive.org/

Keep Indianapolis Beautiful—http://www.kibi.org/

Shepherd Community Center—https://www.shepherdcommunity.org/

Second Helpings—https://www.secondhelpings.org/

Iowa
Families Helping Families of Iowa—http://www.familieshelpingfamiliesofiowa.org/

United Way of Central Iowa—https://www.unitedwaydm.org/

Joppa Kids Homeless Outreach—http://www.joppa.org/joppakids/

Meals from the Heartland—htttp://mealsfromtheheartland.org/

Kansas
Volunteer Kansas—https://www.volunteerkansas.org/

KindCraft—http://kindcraft.org/

KC Pet Project—https://kcpetproject.org/

Harvesters—https://www.harvesters.org/

ServeKC—https://www.meetup.com/ServeKC/

Kentucky
Kentucky Cabinet Health and Family Services—https://chfs.ky.gov/

Kosair Charities—https://kosair.org/

Dare to Care Food Bank—https://daretocare.org/

Jarrett's Joy Cart—http://thejoycart.com/

Louisiana
Volunteer Louisiana—http://www.volunteerlouisiana.gov/

Grow Dat Youth Farm—https://growdatyouthfarm.org/

HandsOn New Orleans—https://www.handsonneworleans.org/

United Way of Southeast Louisiana—http://www.unitedwaysela.org/

NOLA Tree Project—https://nolatreeproject.org/

Audubon Nature Institute—https://audubonnatureinstitute.org/

Youth Rebuilding New Orleans—http://yrno.com/

Maine

Volunteer Maine—http://www.volunteermaine.org/

HandsOn Portland—https://www.handsonportland.org/

Catholic Charities Maine—https://www.ccmaine.org/

Preble Street—https://www.preblestreet.org/

Maryland

Doing Good Together (Baltimore)—https://www.doinggoodtogether.org/family-volunteering-baltimore

Chesapeake Bay Foundation—http://www.cbf.org/

Stella Maris Inc.—https://www.stellamaris.org/

Adopt-a-Road Program—https://www.baltimorecountymd.gov/Agencies/publicworks/highways/adoptaroad.html

Bethesda Cares—www.bethesdacares.org

Massachusetts

Doing Good Together (Boston)—https://www.doinggoodtogether.org/family-volunteering-boston

Project Giving Kids—https://www.projectgivingkids.org/

Catching Joy—http://catchingjoy.org/

Boston Cares—https://www.bostoncares.org/

Community Cooks—https://communitycooks.org/

Cradles to Crayons Giving Factory—https://www.cradlestocrayons.org/boston/

Friends of the Blue Hills—http://friendsofthebluehills.org/

Michigan

Gleaners Community Food Bank—http://www.gcfb.org/

United Way of Washtenaw County—http://www.volunteerwashtenaw.org/

United Way for Southeastern Michigan—https://unitedwaysem.org/

Arts and Scraps—https://www.artsandscraps.org/

Focus Hope—https://www.focushope.edu

Home Fur Ever—http://homefurever.com/

Capuchin Soup Kitchen—http://www.cskdetroit.org/

Minnesota

Doing Good Together (Twin Cities)—https://www.doinggoodtogether.org/family-volunteering-twin-cities

Volunteers Enlisted to Assist People (VEAP)—https://veap.org/

Hunger Solutions Minnesota—http://www.hungersolutions.org/

Animal Humane Society—https://www.animalhumanesociety.org/

Salvation Army Minnesota—https://salvationarmynorth.org/

Mississippi

Operation ShoeString—https://operationshoestring.org/

Volunteer Mississippi—http://www.volunteermississippi.ms.gov/

Mississippi Children's Museum—https://www.mschildrensmuseum.org/

National Park Service (Mississippi)—https://www.nps.gov/miss/

Missouri

Fun 4 St. Louis Kids—http://fun4stlkids.com/

United Way of Greater St. Louis—https://www.stlvolunteer.org/

Interfaith Partnership—http://www.interfaithstl.org/

Missouri Botanical Garden—http://www.missouribotanicalgarden.org/

Montana

Montana State Parks—http://stateparks.mt.gov/volunteer

Montana Natural History Center—http://www.montananaturalist.org/

Montana Wilderness Association—https://wildmontana.org/

City of Great Falls—https://greatfallsmt.net/police/volunteer-program

Global Volunteers—https://globalvolunteers.org/community-projects/ (choose "USA –Montana")

Nebraska

Lutheran Family Services—https://www.lfsneb.org/

Together Omaha—http://togetheromaha.org/

Omaha Against Hunger—https://www.omahaagainsthunger.org/

Promise Ship—https://www.promiseship.org/

Nevada

Nevada Volunteers—http://nevadavolunteers.org/

Spread the Word Nevada—http://spreadthewordnevada.org/

Las Vegas Rescue Mission—https://vegasrescue.org/

Vegas Roots Community Garden—http://vegasroots.org/

Helping Hands of Vegas Valley—http://hhovv.org/

New Hampshire

Volunteer New Hampshire—http://volunternh.org/

New Horizons New Hampshire—https://newhorizonsnh.org/

Blue Ocean Society—http://www.blueoceansociety.org/

Granite United Way—http://www.graniteuw.org/

Children's Museum of New Hampshire—https://www.childrens-museum.org/

New Jersey

Jersey Cares—https://www.jerseycares.org/

Kids to Kids—https://www.kidstokids.us/

America's Grow-a-Row—https://www.americasgrowarow.org/

Bergen Volunteer Center—https://www.bergenvolunteers.org/

Bridges Outreach—http://www.bridgesoutreach.org/

Moms Helping Moms Foundation—https://www.momshelpingmomsfoundation.org/

Pedals for Progress—http://www.p4p.org/

New Mexico

Center for Nonprofit Excellence—https://www.centerfornonprofitexcellence.org/

PullTogether.org—https://pulltogether.org/

United Way of Central New Mexico—https://uwcnm.org/

Animal Humane New Mexico—https://animalhumanenm.org/

City of Albuquerque— http://www.cabq.gov/abq-volunteers/

New York

Doing Good Together (New York City)—https://www.doinggoodtogether.org/family-volunteering-nyc

New York Cares—https://www.newyorkcares.org/volunteering/family-friendly-projects

Lifting Up Westchester—https://www.liftingupwestchester.org/

Dorot—http://www.dorotusa.org/

Citymeals on Wheels—https://www.citymeals.org/

Green Teens—https://www.nycgovparks.org/programs/recreation/teens

Food Bank for New York City—https://www.foodbanknyc.org/

Good+Foundation—https://goodplusfoundation.org/

God's Love We Deliver—https://www.glwd.org/

New York Common Pantry—http://nycommonpantry.org/

North Carolina

HandsOn Charlotte—https://www.handsoncharlotte.org/

Share Charlotte—https://sharecharlotte.org/

Little Helpers (on Facebook)—https://www.facebook.com/LittleHelpersVolunteers/

Activate Good—https://activategood.org/

Community Baby Shower and Give a Kid a Coat—http://www.acleanerworld.com/aboutus/givingback.aspx

Backpack Beginnings—https://backpackbeginnings.org/

Fun 4 Raleigh Kids—http://fun4raleighkids.com/

Diaper Bank of North Carolina—https://ncdiaperbank.org/

Furry Hugs Inc.—http://www.furryhugs.org/

Friendship Gardens—htttp://friendship-gardens.org/

North Dakota
Volunteer Bismarck-Mandan—http://www.volunteerbisman.org/

Great Plains Food Bank—https://www.greatplainsfoodbank.org/

Ohio
Seeds of Caring—https://www.seedsofcaring.org/

Caring Cubs—http://cc1.caringcubs.org/

Stepping Stones—https://steppingstonesohio.org/

See Kids Dream—http://www.seekidsdream.org/

Hilliard Food Pantry—https://www.hilliardfoodpantry.org/

HandsOn Northeast Ohio—https://www.handsonneo.org/

Greater Cleveland Volunteers—http://www.greaterclevelandvolunteers.org/

Project Making Kids Count—https://projectmkc.org/

Oklahoma
ServeOK—http://www.serveok.org/

Caleb's Cause Foundation—http://www.calebscausefoundation.org/

Keep Oklahoma Beautiful—https://www.keepoklahomabeautiful.com/

OKC Beautiful—https://www.okcbeautiful.com/

Hope Center—https://hopecenterofedmond.com/

Best Friends of Pets—https://bestfriendsofpets.org/

Oregon
Little Hands Can—https://littlehandscan.org/

Children's Book Bank—https://www.childrensbookbank.org/

HandsOn Portland—https://www.handsonportland.org/

Friends of Trees—https://friendsoftrees.org/

Store to Door—https://storetodooroforegon.org/

Oregon Food Bank—https://www.oregonfoodbank.org/

Pennsylvania

United Way of Pennsylvania—https://uwswpa.org/

Foster Love Project—http://www.fosterloveproject.org/

Pennsylvania SPCA—https://www.pspca.org/

Philabundance—https://www.philabundance.org/

Youth Volunteer Corp.—https://www.yvcphiladelphia.org/

Rhode Island

United Way of Rhode Island—https://uwri.org/

Animal Rescue Rhode Island—http://www.animalrescueri.org/

Clothes to Kids Rhode Island—http://clothestokidsri.org/

Rhode Island Community Food Bank—https://rifoodbank.org/

South Carolina

Family Connection SC—https://www.familyconnectionsc.org/

United Way of South Carolina—http://www.uwasc.org/

Charleston Animal Society—https://www.charlestonanimalsociety.org/

Low Country Orphan Relief—http://lowcountryorphanrelief.org/

South Dakota

HelpLine Center—http://www.helplinecenter.org/

Feeding South Dakota—https://feedingsouthdakota.org/

Global Volunteers—https://globalvolunteers.org/community-projects/ (choose "USA – South Dakota")

Tennessee

HandsOn Nashville—https://www.hon.org/

Second Harvest Food Bank—https://secondharvestmidtn.org/

Volunteer East Tennessee—https://www.voluneeretn.org/

City of Knoxville—http://www.knoxvilletn.gov/residents/volunteer_opportunities

Mother to Mother—https://mothertomotherinc.org/

Texas

Generation Serve—https://www.generationserve.org/

Wee Volunteer—http://www.weevolunteer.org/

Mission Accomplished: Operation Clean Clothes— http://mission-accomplished.org/portfolio-items/operation-clean-clothes/

Keep Austin Beautiful—https://keepaustinbeautiful.org/

Meals on Wheels and More—https://www.mealsonwheelscentraltexas.org/

Utah

U Serve Utah—https://www.heritage.utah.gov/userveutah

United Way of Utah—http://211utah.org/

Tracy Aviary—https://www.tracyaviary.org/

Community Action Services and Food Bank—http://communityactionprovo.org/

Little Lambs of Utah—http://www.littlelambsofutah.org/

Vermont

United Way of Vermont—https://unitedwaynwvt.org/

Committee on Temporary Shelter—http://cotsonline.org/

Chittenden Emergency Food Shelf—http://www.feedingchittenden.org/

Chittenden Humane Society—https://www.chittendenhumane.org/

Lund—https://lundvt.org/

Old Spokes Home—https://www.oldspokeshome.com/

Vermont Food Bank—https://www.vtfoodbank.org/

Vermont Gleaning Collective—http://www.vermontgleaningcollective.org/

Virginia

Northern Virginia Family Services—https://www.nvfs.org/

Volunteer Fairfax—http://www.volunteerfairfax.org/

Leadership Center for Excellence—http://leadercenter.org/

Action in Community through Service—https://www.actspwc.org/

Volunteer Arlington—https://volunteer.leadercenter.org/

Shelter House, Inc.—http://www.shelterhouse.org/

Housing Families First—http://www.housingfamiliesfirst.org/

Washington

Doing Good Together (Seattle)—https://www.doinggoodtogether.org/family-volunteering-seattle

Solid Ground—https://www.solid-ground.org/

Volunteer Washington—http://www.volunteerwashington.org/

Northwest Harvest—https://www.northwestharvest.org/

Eastside Baby Corner—https://babycorner.org/

West Virginia

Volunteer West Virginia—https://volunteer.wv.gov/

United Way of West Virginia—http://www.unitedwaycwv.org/

Global Volunteers—https://globalvolunteers.org/community-projects/ (choose "USA – West Virginia")

Wisconsin

Sunbeam Kids—https://sunbeamkids.org/

Toddlers and Kids on a Mission—http://toammke.org/

Community Shares of Wisconsin—https://www.communityshares.com/

Middleton Outreach Ministry—http://www.momhelps.org/

Wisconsin Humane Society—http://www.wihumane.org/

Volunteer Wisconsin—http://volunteerwisconsin.org/

Wyoming

Serve Wyoming—http://www.servewyoming.org/

Kindness Ranch Animal Sanctuary—http://www.kindnessranch.org/

United Way of Southwest Wyoming—http://www.swunitedway.org/

District of Columbia

Greater DC Diaper Bank—https://greaterdcdiaperbank.org/

We Are Family DC—http://www.wearefamilydc.org/

ALIVE! Food Distribution—https://www.alive-inc.org/

Charles E. Smith Life Communities—https://www.smithlifecommunities.org/

Lucky Dog Animal Rescue—https://www.luckydoganimalrescue.org/home

Capital Area Food Bank—https://www.capitalareafoodbank.org/

Kindness Opportunities in Canada

Plan Canada—https://plancanada.ca/

Volunteer Toronto—https://www.volunteertoronto.ca/

WE—https://www.we.org/

Project Sunshine Canada—https://projectsunshine.ca/home/

BabyGoRound—http://www.babygoround.ca/

The Backpacks 101 Project—http://backpacks101.blogspot.com/

Food 4 Kids Ontario—https://www.food4kids.ca/

Ve'Ahavta—https://veahavta.org/

REFERENCES

Alston-Able, Nicole, and Virginia Berninger. 2018. "Relationships Between Home Literacy Practices and School Achievement: Implications for Consultation and Home-School Collaboration." *Journal of Educational and Psychological Consultation* 28(2): 164–189.

Compassion International. 2018. "World Days: International Children's Day." Compassion International. https://www.compassion.com/world-days/international-childrens-day.htm

Corporation for National and Community Service. n.d. "September 11th National Day of Service and Remembrance." Corporation for National and Community Service. https://www.nationalservice.gov/special-initiatives/days-service/september-11th-national-day-service-and-remembrance

Cox, Meg. 2003. *The Book of New Family Traditions: How to Create Great Rituals for Holidays and Every Day*. Philadelphia, PA: Running Press.

Domonoske, Camila. 2016. "Refugees, Displaced People Surpass 60 Million for First Time, UNHCR Says." NPR. https://www.npr.org/sections/thetwo-way/2016/06/20/482762237/refugees-displaced-people-surpass-60-million-for-first-time-unhcr-says

Eckart, Kim. 2017. "How Reading and Writing with Your Child Boost More Than Just Literacy." UW News. https://www.washington.edu/news/2017/08/28/how-reading-and-writing-with-your-child-boost-more-than-just-literacy/

Editors of Encyclopedia Britannica. 2018. "Diwali: Hindu Festival." Encyclopedia Britannica. https://www.britannica.com/topic/Diwali-Hindu-festival

Freeman, Michael. 2018. "Guidance for Honoring Veterans with Grave Site Flags on Memorial Day." Bryan on Scouting: A Blog for the BSA's Adult Leaders. https://blog.scoutingmagazine.org/2018/05/22/honoring-veterans-with-gravesite-flags-memorial-day/

Friedman, Jenny, and Jolene Roehlkepartain. 2010. *Doing Good Together: 101 Easy, Meaningful Service Projects for Families, Schools, and Communities*. Minneapolis, MN: Free Spirit.

Galinsky, Ellen. 1999. *Ask the Children: What America's Children Really Think About Working Parents*. New York, NY: William Morrow.

Ibham, Manal. 2018. "Do Muslims Pay Zakat Only in Ramadan?" Global Sadaqah. https://www.globalsadaqah.com/blog/muslims-pay-zakat-ramadan/

Karenga, Maulana. 2016. "Kwanzaa: A Brief Description." Official Kwanzaa Website. http://www.officialkwanzaawebsite.org/images/Kwanzaa--ABriefDescription2016.jpg

Kaur, Tarandip. 2017. "Festival of Lights: All You Need to Know About Diwali." Forbes. https://www.forbes.com/sites/tarandipkaur/2017/10/18/festival-of-lights-all-you-need-to-know-about-diwali/#26f673bf4678

Making Caring Common Project. 2014. *Executive Summary.* Cambridge, MA: Harvard Graduate School of Education. https://mcc.gse.harvard.edu/files/gse-mcc/files/mcc-research-report.pdf

Minnaert, Lynn. 2015. *US Family Travel Survey September 2015.* New York, NY: Family Travel Association and NYU School of Professional Studies. https://www.researchgate.net/publication/282365757_2015_US_Family_Travel_Survey

Muslim Aid. 2017. "Zakat and Sadaqah." Muslim Aid. https://www.muslimaid.org/media-centre/blog/zakat-and-sadaqah/

No Kid Hungry. 2018. "Hunger Facts." No Kid Hungry. https://www.nokidhungry.org/who-we-are/hunger-facts

Office of Public and Intergovernmental Affairs. 2015. "History of Veterans Day." US Department of Veterans Affairs. https://www.va.gov/opa/vetsday/vetdayhistory.asp

Official Kwanzaa Website. 2018. "Fundamental Questions About Kwanzaa: An Interview." Official Kwanzaa Website. http://www.officialkwanzaawebsite.org/faq.shtml

Official Kwanzaa Website. 2018. "Nguzo Saba: The Seven Principles." Official Kwanzaa Website. http://www.officialkwanzaawebsite.org/NguzoSaba.shtml

Quindlen, Anna. 2000. "Goodbye Dr. Spock." AnnaQuindlen.net. http://annaquindlen.net/goodbye-dr-spock/

Radez, Wes. 2018. "How to Celebrate Chinese New Year." Chinese American Family. http://www.chineseamericanfamily.com/chinese-new-year/

Rock, Amanda. 2017. "Kwanzaa Traditions for Kids and Families." Verywell Family. https://www.verywellfamily.com/kwanzaa-traditions-for-kids-and-families-2765149

Rubin, Gretchen. 2015. *The Happiness Project: Or, Why I Spent a Year Trying to Sing in the Morning, Clean My Closets, Fight Right, Read Aristotle, and Generally Have More Fun.* Rev. ed. New York, NY: Harper.

Suizzo, Marie-Anne. 2007. "Parents' Goals and Values for Children: Dimensions of Independence and Interdependence across Four US Ethnic Groups." *Journal of Cross-Cultural Psychology* 38(4): 506–530.

Suri, Manveena. 2018. "Why India Celebrates Holi: The Legends behind the Festival of Color." CNN. https://edition.cnn.com/2018/03/01/asia/india-holi-explainer-intl/index.html

US Department of Labor. n.d. "History of Labor Day." US Department of Labor. https://www.dol.gov/general/laborday/history

Varner, Joyce. 2005. "The Elder Orphans: Who Are They?" *The Alabama Nurse* 32(3): 19–20.

INDEX